T0372362

Cambridge Elements ≡

Elements in Anthropological Archaeology in the 21st Century
edited by
Eli Dollarhide
New York University Abu Dhabi
Michael Galaty
University of Michigan
Junko Habu
University of California, Berkeley
Patricia A. McAnany
University of North Carolina at Chapel Hill
John K. Millhauser
North Carolina State University
Rita Wright
New York University

IDENTITY STUDIES
IN ARCHAEOLOGY

Emma Blake
School of Anthropology, University of Arizona

CAMBRIDGE
UNIVERSITY PRESS

Shaftesbury Road, Cambridge CB2 8EA, United Kingdom

One Liberty Plaza, 20th Floor, New York, NY 10006, USA

477 Williamstown Road, Port Melbourne, VIC 3207, Australia

314–321, 3rd Floor, Plot 3, Splendor Forum, Jasola District Centre,
New Delhi – 110025, India

103 Penang Road, #05–06/07, Visioncrest Commercial, Singapore 238467

Cambridge University Press is part of Cambridge University Press & Assessment,
a department of the University of Cambridge.

We share the University's mission to contribute to society through the pursuit of
education, learning and research at the highest international levels of excellence.

www.cambridge.org
Information on this title: www.cambridge.org/9781009459754

DOI: 10.1017/9781009459747

© Emma Blake 2024

This publication is in copyright. Subject to statutory exception and to the provisions
of relevant collective licensing agreements, no reproduction of any part may take
place without the written permission of Cambridge University Press & Assessment.

When citing this work, please include a reference to the DOI 10.1017/9781009459747

First published 2024

A catalogue record for this publication is available from the British Library.

ISBN 978-1-009-45975-4 Hardback
ISBN 978-1-009-45970-9 Paperback
ISSN 2753-6327 (online)
ISSN 2753-6319 (print)

Cambridge University Press & Assessment has no responsibility for the persistence
or accuracy of URLs for external or third-party internet websites referred to in this
publication and does not guarantee that any content on such websites is, or will
remain, accurate or appropriate.

Identity Studies in Archaeology

Elements in Anthropological Archaeology in the 21st Century

DOI: 10.1017/9781009459747
First published online: November 2024

Emma Blake
School of Anthropology, University of Arizona

Author for correspondence: Emma Blake, ecblake@arizona.edu

Abstract: This Element explores the origins, current state, and future of the archaeological study of identity. A floruit of scholarship in the late twentieth century introduced identity as a driving force in society, and archaeologists sought expressions of gender, status, ethnicity, and more in the material remains of the past. A robust consensus emerged about identity and its characteristics: dynamic; contested; context-driven; performative; polyvalent; and intersectional. From the early 2000s, identity studies were challenged by new theories of materiality and ontology on the one hand, and by an influx of new data from bioarchaeology on the other. Yet identity studies have proven remarkably enduring. Through European case studies from prehistory to the present, this Element charts identity's evolving place in anthropological archaeology.

Keywords: archaeology, identity, bioarchaeology, posthumanism, Europe

© Emma Blake 2024

ISBNs: 9781009459754 (HB), 9781009459709 (PB), 9781009459747 (OC)
ISSNs: 2753-6327 (online), 2753-6319 (print)

Contents

1 Introduction

The identification of peoples of the past is fundamental to the archaeological endeavor, as the field is understood by the public and by its practitioners. For almost thirty years, questions of origins and descriptions of personal and group characteristics have been posed and answered in a particular way, drawing on a fairly uniform understanding of what identity is and how it works, one that differed from earlier, ascriptive approaches. Beginning in the early aughts, there were stirrings of discontent in theoretical archaeology even as identity studies were reaching their apex in popularity. Within a decade, identity was virtually supplanted among theorists by various new approaches that can be collectively labeled posthumanism. At the same moment that identity was declining in theoretical circles, however, advances in archaeological science provided rich new data with which to understand identities in the past. These advances, a veritable revolution, were in the field of bioarchaeology, the study of human remains. Bioarchaeology includes traditional osteological work, as well as the biochemistry methods that are transforming the discipline, notably aDNA and stable isotope analysis.[1] Drawing on case studies from European prehistory, this Element charts the past, present, and future of identity studies in archaeology. In the normal order of things, identity would have fallen universally out of favor in lockstep with the theoretical vanguard. Instead, it has experienced a different trajectory from other research themes. First, the advent of these technologies which are directly applicable to questions of identity has halted its decline. Second, identity theory's resonance with a public steeped in identity politics aids in its endurance. From the beginning, archaeological studies of identity were fueled and reinforced by broader societal interest in identity politics. This public interest continues more forcefully than ever in movements for LGBTQIA+ rights, BIPOC rights, #MeToo, and BlackLivesMatter movements. These currents running through popular culture contribute to identity theory's enduring relevance in archaeology in spite of claims of its demise from the theorists.

Definitions of this complex word "identity" abound, but the OED offers, among several options, "a set of characteristics or a description that distinguishes a person or thing from others." This definition approximates how the term is applied in archaeology, although we would substitute "groups" for "thing." This uniformity in archaeological identity studies avoided the disputes over definitions and applications of identity occurring elsewhere in academe:

---

[1] While archaeogeneticists may bristle at their work on aDNA being subsumed into bioarchaeology, I contend that their data, in a literal sense of being derived from human remains, belong intellectually if not disciplinarily under that umbrella.

Brubaker and Cooper (2000: 6–8) enumerate five broad uses and meanings, often contradictory, of the term, but in archaeology, there were few arguments over semantics. Identity in modern archaeological usage has some distinct characteristics: It is dynamic; contested; context-driven; performative; polyvalent; and intersectional. This understanding of identity has proven to be supple and expansive enough to work in most archaeological settings. By "work" I mean here that the answers to the who? questions sound reasonable to archaeologists, fit with other contemporary archaeological research, and in many respects echo popular cultural perspectives on identity.

The Element presents a wide range of examples, and a map is provided indicating the locations of sites (Figure 1). In addition, three iconic European case studies from different periods are evoked on multiple occasions. The oldest case study of the three is the 31,000-year-old Gravettian period triple burial at Dolní Věstonice, Moravia, Czech Republic (Svoboda 2020). The site is an open-air settlement (occupied for repeated short intervals) with associated burials. The inhumations in question, discovered during excavations in 1986, consist of two bodies (DV 13 and DV 14) flanking a central body (DV 15) (Figure 2). The left individual (DV 13) was purposefully arranged with their hand resting on DV 15's pubic area, while the right individual (DV 14) was buried face down with their left arm draped over DV 15's right arm. Spruce branches were spread over the corpses, and ochre covered their faces and DV15's pubic area. The Dolní Věstonice triple burials offer a rare chance to explore identities and symbolic behavior in hunter-gatherer populations of the Paleolithic.

Ötzi the Iceman, the anachronistic but humanizing name for the 5,200-year-old frozen body found at 3,200 m a.s.l. in the Tyrolean Alps in 1991, is another case study (see Spindler 1995 for the first-hand account of discovery and early study). He is the best preserved human mummified corpse of that period in the world (Figure 3). Because after death his body was buried by snow and ice through natural processes, a remarkable amount of soft tissue was preserved, and some of his gear, including his trousers, shoes, backpack, and other possessions, also survived. Since his discovery, he has been studied using every method one can think of; Ötzi is an archaeological cottage industry in his own right. The abundance of data derived from Ötzi means that archaeologists treat him simultaneously as a unicum and as a representative of his time; therein some interesting tensions lie.

The "bell beaker phenomenon" as it is now called began some 500 years after Ötzi lived (Brodie 1997). Briefly, ceramic jars (beakers) whose shape recalls a bell are common grave goods in third millennium BCE burials across a swathe of Western and Central Europe that extends from Poland and Hungary in the

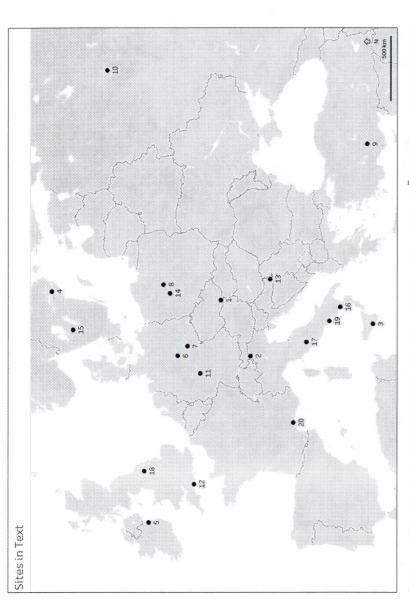

Figure 1 Map of sites mentioned in the text. 1. Dolní Věstonice, Moravia, Czech Republic; 2. Ötzi the Iceman's findspot; 3. Butera, Sicily; 4. Birka, Sweden; 5. Newgrange, Ireland; 6. Benzingerode, Germany; 7. Eulau, Germany; 8. Krusza Zamkowa, Poland; 9. Çatalhöyük, Turkey; 10. Sunghir, Russia; 11. Glauberg, Germany; 12. Poundbury Camp, England; 13. Nuštar, Croatia; 14. Giecz, Poland; 15. Falbygden, Sweden; 16. Romito Cave, Italy; 17. Poggio Gramignano, Italy; 18. Driffield Terrace, York, England; 19. Pompeii, Italy; and 20. Lattes (ancient Lattara), France. Map by V. Moses.

Figure 2 The 31,000-year-old triple burial at Dolní Věstonice II, Moravia, Czech Republic. From Left to Right: DV 13, DV 15, and DV 14.   © 2016 Mittnik et al. Creative Commons – Attribution 4.0 International – CC BY 4.0

east to Iberia in the southwest and Britain and southern Scandinavia in the north (Figures 4 and 5). One of the fundamental debates in European prehistory, in full swing for over a century, is if the pan-European presence of these distinct pottery vessels in Late Neolithic/Copper Age mortuary contexts constitutes the spread of an actual ethnic group, a common set of beliefs, or something else. The progress of beaker research tracks well with the evolution of studies of cultural identity. These three case studies illuminate key aspects of identity studies and they are revisited at various points in the text.

1.1 A Robust Consensus

Although studying objects to reveal the people who made, used, and left them behind has been fundamental to archaeology since the field's inception, the recent approach to identity was utterly different from how identity had been treated by archaeologists through much of the twentieth century. In the culture-historical phase of scholarship, archaeological cultures and social status were the only identity categories of interest, and these were viewed as fixed, innate, and ascribed, that is, "socially constructed on the basis of the contingencies of birth" (Jenkins 1996: 142). People would make and use and do things in a manner characteristic of their ethnicity and station in life, and thus the archaeological record would reflect those past identities. It was straightforward

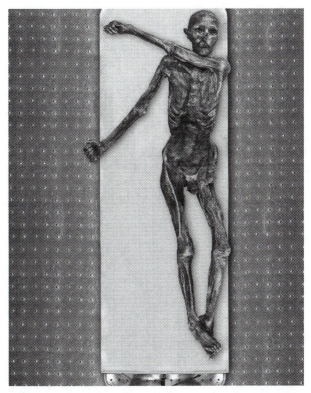

Figure 3 Ötzi the Iceman, the 5,200-year-old body found in the Tyrolean Alps, Italy. © South Tyrol Museum of Archaeology – www.iceman.it

work, undergirded by the assurance of "the correlation of distinctive cultural habits and ways of life with discrete communities or cultural groups" (Jones 1997: 17). Being a woman or a Roman or a peasant or a member of a particular kin group was nonnegotiable. People of the past could thus be identified the way a pot could be identified, as a sum of fixed categories: sixth-century BCE Athenian black-figure amphora and sixth-century Athenian affluent adult male. In fact gender was not a subject of interest, beyond basic identifications: female skeletons could be differentiated from males by pelvis shape and associated grave goods and some heteronormative assumptions about universal behaviors (e.g. women were child-rearers; men were buried with weapons). Ethnic groups would reveal themselves through geographically and temporally bounded artifact types which themselves coalesce into archaeological cultures; the fancier the grave/dwelling/possessions, the higher status the individual . . . identity was simple.

Figure 4 Ceramic bell beaker. Prov. Folkestone, England. Acq. 1955 British Museum. Object number 1955,0703.1 © The Trustees of the British Museum

From the 1960s, the processual movement rejected the culture-history approach, but identity itself was not a topic of interest, beyond a dismissal of the ethnohistorical method of projecting back to past peoples on the expectation of the stability of modern cultural boundaries. Other valences of identity were largely undertheorized although feminist archaeology emerged in the era of processualism. While outside archaeology postmodern approaches were taking hold in academia, it was not until the early 1990s, especially within the new theoretical paradigm of post-processualism but not exclusively, that the traditional ascriptive approach to identities fell out of favor in Anglo-American archaeology. The new understanding of identity was not as a static condition of given attributes that coalesce into an inert label, such as female or French or old, but as instead the product of negotiated self-ascription and of the imposition of constructed labels by others. Jenkins (1996: 20) puts it this way: "Individuals are unique and variable, but selfhood is thoroughly socially constructed: in the processes of primary and secondary socialisation, and in the ongoing processes

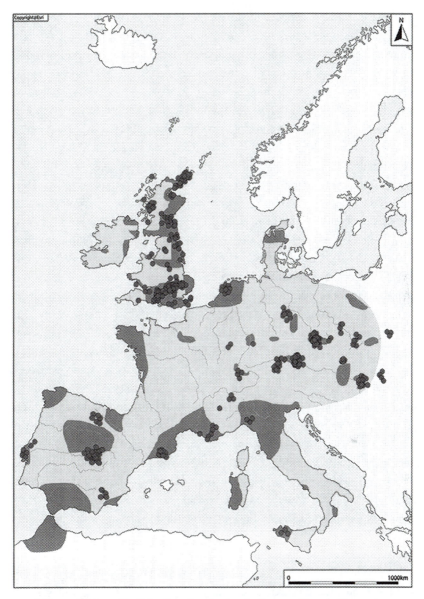

Figure 5 Map of bell beaker distribution in Europe (dots indicate sites where aDNA was obtained). Reprinted from Cambridge University Press on behalf of Antiquity Publications Ltd © 2021 I. Armit and D. Reich (figure 2, by R. Kershaw). Creative Commons – Attribution 4.0 International – CC BY 4.0

of social interaction within which individuals define and redefine themselves and others throughout their lives." According to this framing, identities – both group and individual – change depending on circumstance, they are not monolithic, they are instruments of power (over and to). Furthermore, they are relational, or extrinsic, meaningful only in comparison to others, rather than being intrinsically held. The 1989 publication of Steven Shennan's edited volume "Archaeological Approaches to Cultural Identity" is as good an event as any to mark the beginning of the new identity studies in the discipline. The identity consensus that arose on the wave of post processual agency-based approaches depended on two key premises: a constructivist view in which identity is intentional and agent-driven, and, crucially for archaeologists, that purposive identity-driven actions, and the struggles to express or suppress identities of self and others, would leave traces in the archaeological record.

While identity had been a buzzword in the social sciences since the 1960s (see Brubaker and Cooper 2000 for a brief history), archaeological interest in identity was most directly inspired by the work of several scholars outside archaeology whose reach stretched across the academy. At the risk of oversimplifying a complex story, key influences on archaeological approaches to ethnicity were Fredrik Barth's 1969 edited volume, *Ethnic Groups and Boundaries*, particularly his introduction; for identity politics and the real and symbolic violence of othering there was Edward Said's (1978) *Orientalism*; for gender an inspiration was Judith Butler's body of work crystallizing in *Gender Trouble* (1990); and for social class, Pierre Bourdieu's 1979 *Distinction* was a central text. Bourdieu's *Outline of a Theory of Practice* (1977), a foundational text for agency studies and practice theory, was also critical for identity studies as agent-based approaches were intertwined with identity studies: indeed, agency was perceived as the engine in identity assertions, while identity was a catalyst for individual agents to act. These source texts in some cases were written decades before they found real purchase in archaeological theory. Disparate as they are, all argue that the way humans arrange themselves and others into groups is not innate or natural but is the product of ongoing struggles for power and advantage. Archaeology's absorption of these approaches, sometimes in watered-down versions, was a response to a series of flash points within the field: feminist archaeologists protesting the erasure of women from the past; a wholesale rejection of the culture-history approach and the nationalisms arising from ethnic primordialism; and a postcolonial call to recenter and validate the marginalized and conquered.

The first spark to ignite archaeological identity studies came from feminist archaeologists drawing attention to the deletion of and biases against women in standard androcentric analyses of the archaeological record on the one hand,

and their own subjection to sexist treatment in the workplace on the other. The catalyst was Conkey and Spector's (1984) article, "Archaeology and the study of gender." Gender studies were thus at the forefront of identity work. From early corrective approaches to the past flippantly summarized as "add women and stir," they expanded to encompass a rejection of heteronormative narratives of the past and an acknowledgment of diverse and fluid cultural constructions of gender, queer identities, and eventually biological sex itself. Identity studies absorbed from queer theory the notion that social norms are defined in opposition to deviance of all kinds, sexual included. Voss's (2008: 328) assertion that "Sexes, genders, and sexualities are thus negotiated through an ongoing dance of identification and misidentification" captures the way in which current trends in gender and queer archaeologies align with identity studies. The relationship between feminist archaeology and queer archaeologies is not without tension: "queer theory's focus on the deconstruction of gender and sexuality represents a direct challenge to a feminist practice concerned with legitimizing gender studies" (Blackmore 2011: 78; see also Meskell 1996; Voss 2000). The recent term "engendered archaeology," which inserts gender as a structuring principle rather than an axis of difference in competition with other identity axes, may thread this needle (Montón-Subías and Meyer 2014).

Critiques of ethnicity were another entry point for identity studies. The Oxford English Dictionary sidesteps the complexities of this category, defining ethnicity as: "Status in respect of membership of a group regarded as ultimately of common descent, or having a common national or cultural tradition." In practice, ethnicity, because it is based on a group's self-perception, is impossible to square with the archaeological record. Ethnic groups rely on a social memory of a common origin that is perceived as geographic and genetic, and while that does not make the present-day ethnicity any less real, the perceived origins are always to some degree fictive. Furthermore, in prehistoric contexts without attestation that a group self-identified as "ethnic," the exercise is futile. Despite the difficulties, ethnicity has been a perennial subject in prehistoric archaeology from the nineteenth century, and it took a while for archaeologists to absorb the message of cultural anthropology that there is no easy way to detect temporally and geographically bounded ethnic groups because such groups do not exist (Barth 1969). In Europe a critique of ethnic primordialism from another angle, this time highlighting its role in Nazi propaganda (Arnold 1990) and in other irredentist claims, has demonstrated that an archaeology of traditional ethnicity is not just impossible but dangerous. Archaeological studies of the origins of ethnic identities can have real-world consequences, playing into modern-day conflicts by perceived descendent communities (for the early literature on this, see the papers in Meskell 2002). Insoll (2007: 7) describes how archaeologists have avoided identifying and labeling ancient ethnic groups from the material record in Sudan out of concern that the data could be weaponized by contemporary groups in the midst of conflict. This is not to say that archaeology cannot address ethnicity under some circumstances: indeed the instrumentalist understanding of ethnicity, that it is context-driven, performed, and negotiated, makes it well-suited to archaeological research (Jones 1997; Blake 2014). Archaeology can assist in exposing the performative components of ethnicity formation and maintenance, often conveyed through things and places, as well as the catalysts for ethnicity formation. But instrumentalist readings of ethnicity are not without controversy, especially when they conflict with primordialist self-ascriptions of indigenous groups whose claims can afford them some real advantages (Gil-White 1999). Given the complexities, I will be using the less loaded term cultural identity here unless speaking directly about studies of ethnicity.

Third, the scrutiny of the real and symbolic violence of European colonialism has rebounded through archaeology, and an interest in subaltern groups in postcolonial studies was refracted in archaeology through the lens of identity. Postcolonial approaches in archaeology have emphasized how constructions of race and nationality have riven populations and justified everything from discrimination to outright bloodshed. Strongly influenced by Said's work, recognition of archaeology's complicity in the perpetuation of racial stereotypes began by the late 1980s (e.g. Larsen 1989). From the postcolonial literature, a rich set of terms to describe the struggles at identity expression and construction in situations of culture contact and domination has entered the archaeological lexicon: creolization; hybridity; discrepant identities, the Middle Ground, and period-specific -izations: Romanization, Hellenization, and Celticization. Postcolonial approaches were applied enthusiastically to any population encounter one can name in ancient Europe: from the spread of farming in the Neolithic (Borić 2005) to Greek-native interactions in Italy and Sicily (Malkin 1998; Hodos 2006), the Phoenicians in Iberia (López Ruíz 2021); the Celts in Transylvania (Berecki 2014), and perhaps most of all, to the Roman Empire (e.g. Laurence and Berry 1998).

Postcolonial studies in archaeology fit within a long tradition of work on social hierarchies and status, whether to determine the structure of a given society, or to examine a particular faction within it: A thru-line across disparate studies was the construction of social difference. Identity studies provided a way to speak about those with limited archaeological visibility and even less representation in texts. In the 1980s and 1990s these studies could be Marxist-infused, in both Europe and the U.S. In American historical archaeology Marxist approaches to class were well articulated (see Leone 1984;

McGuire 1992), and now historical archaeologists engage with intersections of class with other axes of difference. In European archaeology, postcolonial studies meant that status was examined with cultural identity in ancient colonial and imperial contexts. Besides the Roman provinces, where a determinant of status was the performance or suppression of indigeneity and Romanness (Mattingly 2014), Iron Age (Hallstatt) Europe offers intriguing examples of the impact of Greek drinking paraphernalia on local political hierarchies: most well-known are the Vix and Hochdorf burials (Arnold 1999; Dietler 1999). Exposing the arbitrary nature of social divisions, and the artifice used to shore up inequities – racial, colonial, and economic – is central to archaeological identity studies.

These separate strands fused by the mid 1990s into identity studies as we understand them, with archaeologists taking on multiple axes of identity at once (see Meskell 2001 for a call to arms). The "big three" axes were ethnicity, social status, and gender, but archaeologists also examined age and childhood (Moore and Scott 1997; Gilchrist 2000; Baxter 2022) sexuality (Voss 2008) as well as community (Canuto and Yaeger 2000), religion (Rebillard 2015), caste (Jamieson 2005), kin (Souvatzi 2017), disability (Hubert 2001), and occupation (Flohr 2017). Fogelin (2019) summarizes the work on identities as "Archaeologies of the Screwed Over," given the emphasis on centering and amplifying the voices of marginalized groups, past and present. Indeed, identity studies in archaeology are generally studies of identity *politics*, looking at questions of power and autonomy to define oneself. Over time, archaeological identity studies expanded, always with the aims of further re-positioning marginalized groups and categories, fine-tuning an agreed-upon concept, and of greater reflexive scrutiny by the scholars doing the studies. As a catch-all explanation for the maintenance of traditional practices, foodways, and clothing, for example, identity was an easy fit, in Europe as elsewhere (Graves-Brown et al. 1996). Although the "pots equal people" aphorism was roundly rejected, studies did rest on the expectation that material culture could be an expression of identity – indeed, more than that, *created* identity, especially in charged contexts.

Working with multiple valences proved difficult, however. Identity studies typically have managed to juggle two or three valences at most, with gender archaeologists leading the way in examining gender in conjunction with status, or ethnicity, or occupation (see papers in Wright 1996). Scholars eventually engaged with a watered-down form of intersectionality, acknowledging poly-valent identities, and recognizing that categories of ethnicity, gender, age, status, and more are all simultaneously present in an individual. But intersectionality, a theory of the multiple components of individuals and the constraints placed on them by external labels, has not been effectively applied, at least as it was intended by the person who coined the term, Kimberlé Crenshaw. Crenshaw (1989: 149) argued that the reduction of composite identities to a list of particular categories is doomed to failure, because this work cannot account for the complex experience of all those categories at work together – the sum is greater than the parts, and not just that, it is *different* than its parts. The implications for archaeology are significant: In a study of, say, elite Gallo-Roman women in the second century CE, even in our combination of descriptive categories we are engaged in reduction and therefore performing symbolic violence against our subject. It is perhaps for this reason that intersectionality is rarely applied explicitly in archaeology, with the exception of historical archaeology, where Black feminist scholars and others have engaged with and adapted Crenshaw's original conception of intersectionality to encompass other intersecting valences and the power dynamics shaping them (see Franklin 2001; Brandon 2004; and articles in Spencer-Wood et al. 2022). Indeed, historical archaeologists have fruitfully engaged with identity studies in ways that far surpass the work of prehistorians, thanks to a rich material and textual record with which to examine multiple and changing axes of difference through different material media (e.g. Reckner and Brighton 1999; Jamieson 2005).

Early identity studies were optimistic in their emphasis on microexpressions of self in the face of oppression. In a study of Romano-British tombstones, for example, Hope (1997: 257) sees their carved portraits as aiding in the formation of the deceased's status: "The funerary monuments construct the identity of those commemorated through a Roman medium and for differing reasons advertise a perceived or desired superiority over others." This would have been particularly important, Hope contends, because the people in question were outsiders, transplants to Britain with little social capital. There is a happy ending: "To these immigrants, who dwelt on the margins of acceptance, the funerary memorial created a sense of permanence and legitimacy not always achieved in life." (257–58). However naïve this may sound now, studies such as this resolved the problem of how to see agency at work among people other than the "big men of history": now even average folk could have a goal, self-expression, and we could see this in their stuff.

While it is reasonable that something as public-facing, permanent, and highly personal as a tombstone would be an opportunity for plugging one's (wished for) identity, some theorists went further to imply that identity construction was happening everywhere. As Insoll (2007: 14) put it, "The archaeology of identities is essentially concerned with the complex process of attempting to recover an insight into the generation of self at a variety of levels: as an individual, within a community, and in public and private contexts." While Insoll acknowledged the limits placed on identity by biology, and the existence and power of externally ascribed identities, there was nonetheless an implication that if we looked hard enough, no matter how circumscribed people's lives were, some wiggle room would have allowed for personal empowerment and self-expression. While the point can seem somewhat academic in European prehistoric contexts, the problems are clear when the history is fresh. This expectation of self-expression in material form was built into some archaeological studies of enslaved people in the American South, where burials, cooking practices, and structured deposits were scrutinized for traces of a carefully curated African legacy (e.g. Ferguson 1992; Handler 1997). This focus on African survivals among enslaved peoples pre-emancipation can risk painting too rosy a picture of the experience of enslavement, one that lets the enslavers off the hook from the desocialization caused by slavery: bluntly put, if the enslaved peoples could still express themselves, they had some autonomy, so it wasn't so bad (see Jamieson 1995: 41 for a clear articulation of the critique). Furthermore, when African elements are missing from enslaved people's assemblages, does that indicate a loss of heritage, and therefore victimization, or does it signal enslaved peoples' innovation and adaptation to changed circumstances? (Jamieson 1995). The interpretations are fraught. In Europe approaches to circumstances of extreme power differentials were framed for a time in terms of resistance (see chapters in Miller et al. 1989), but more common are studies like the abovementioned Hope (1997), with an apolitical emphasis on agency and working within a colonial system (but see Roymans 2019 for an unsanitized take on the violence of Roman conquest).

Identity's success can also be attributed to its easy integration with other bodies of theory, and its applicability to numerous material media. Beyond individual objects, the evidence for identities in the past has come from mortuary contexts but also architecture and the structure of domestic space, with spatial syntax studies offering insights into gender dynamics within households (see Nevett 2001 for an example of tracing women's movements through the Classical Greek house). The placement and arrangement of kitchens can reveal the status of food producers (LeCount 2010). Indeed, much interesting work occurs at the intersection of food studies and identity, with a particular emphasis on food and social structure. Archaeological studies of luxury foods (Ervynck et al. 2003; van der Veen 2003), the social role of drinking (Dietler 2006), and feasting as a means of creating and performing status (Hayden 2001, 2014) have offered insights into how foodways contribute to the construction of identity.

Theories of communities of practice described situated learning from which particular social identities could emerge (Wenger 1998; in ethnoarchaeology, even earlier: e.g. Herbich 1987); studies of landscape, monuments, place, and phenomenology tied in neatly with identity studies in the emphasis on the bodily lived experiences of spaces as constituting identities (Barrett et al. 1991; Thomas 1996; Ashmore and Knapp 1999). Memory studies explored collective memory's central role in forging and cementing group unity (Connerton 1989). These studies recognized that the root of conflict is often contested history, and that opposing groups will draw on counter-memories to mobilize resistance, certainly in nation-states but in other political contexts as well (Galaty 2018). The reuse and resignification of older buildings and monuments were viewed as identity-driven. From Byzantines engaging with a glorified Roman past through spoliation (Papalexandrou 2003), to Anglo-Saxons evoking their distant homeland by burying their dead in familiar Neolithic barrows (Williams 1998), to the heirlooms that confer kin membership on their possessors (Lillios 1999), identity was the impetus for the manipulation of memory through material culture (Van Dyke and Alcock 2003). While archaeologists find these traces of memory work often by clear anachronisms in the archaeological record, such as the reuse of extant buildings or older objects in graves, what contemporary memory studies have shown is that such manipulations of memory can begin almost immediately, in conditions of popular unrest (e.g. contested accounts of Bloody Sunday: Conway 2003). Whether or not the fervently held social memories accurately recall past events, or whether they are instances of Hobsbawm and Ranger's (1983) invented traditions, the recognition that all social memory requires work to be maintained and disseminated echoes scholarship on the construction and maintenance of group identities.

1.2 Early Critiques

Identity's vast scope and easy pairing with other theoretical strands of post-processualism made it well suited to edited volumes, Casella and Fowler (2005), Díaz-Andreu et al. (2005), Insoll (2007), Elliott (2011), Amundsen-Meyer et al. (2011), Ginn et al. (2014), and Campbell et al. (2016), to name a few. These approaches cemented into a consensus surrounding the concept of identity in academic archaeology, with only some muted critiques. Outside the field, Brubaker and Cooper's (2000) article has remained impactful. The authors called out the contradictory notions of identity in academia, in which "soft" identity is contingent, negotiated, and malleable, while the hard version recognizes objective criteria of sameness in groups and well-defined boundaries between members and nonmembers. The hard version of identity "is something people (and groups) can have without being aware of it," and "thus replicates the Marxian epistemology of class" (Brubaker and Cooper 2000: 10). Brubaker and Cooper (2000: 10–11) note that while the soft versions of identity predominate in academia (and here archaeology is no different), in everyday life strong definitions prevail. This is perhaps most evident with nationalism. Duval (1989) examines the case of France, where the Iron Age Gauls are seen as the ancestors of modern French people, despite demographic shifts in the intervening millennia that negate a thru-line from the Gauls to the present-day population.

However the archaeologists are not always the neutral arbiters of truth on matters of national origins. In the case of Greece, Greenberg and Hamilakis (2022) discuss how the links between current inhabitants of a land and a distant past can be established from the top down, with archaeologists and politicians collaborating to fuse disparate peoples into a tidy national identity. In settler societies of the Americas and Oceania with indigenous descendent communities, archaeologists can cause further disruptions. Already damaged by centuries of mistreatment at the hands of European settlers, when indigenous groups claim an ethnic identity and feel a deep affinity to ancestral peoples, the archaeologists' instrumentalist views of historically contingent identities can undermine hard-won indigenous rights. The contradictions take concrete form in debates over object repatriation and indigenous land claims. The latter can be particularly problematic as they tend to rest on exactly the primordialist evocations of place that ostensibly archaeologists now repudiate. On the one hand, as noted above, current approaches to identity dismiss claims based on who has the deepest roots in a place, the purest bloodlines, or the longest memories. On the other, soft, instrumentalist notions of identity can undercut the appeals of victims of land dispossession: in recognizing indigenous peoples as being as dynamic and modern as the settler populations, their authenticity (as popularly understood) is called into question and they lose their leverage in the battles over heritage (de la Cadena and Starn 2007). Lilley (2006) has suggested reframing dispossessed indigenous peoples as diasporic, as distant from their originally configured homeland as any community geographically exiled from their home country. We return to migration and diasporic identities in Section 3.7.

Brubaker and Cooper recommended that what we call identity be broken down into multiple terms for specific phenomena, such as self-understanding and identification. There is merit to this: while the identification of Ötzi the Iceman, in the sense of categories to which he belongs, is possible, it seems altogether reasonable that we cannot get at Ötzi's self-understanding. The subject of collective identities that are negotiated and constructed may be better understood as a process of *identification*, which captures the dynamic, unresolved character of these efforts, rather than the static term identity.

Other critiques of identity studies centered on methods: How exactly to go about drawing links between identity and material culture? Peter Wells'

(2001: 25) observation that "we cannot assume a recurrent consistent correlation between a particular kind of material culture and a specific identity" carried weight, and recurred in discussions of the polysemy of material culture (e.g. Casella and Fowler 2005: 4). This point did not undermine identity studies, however: scholars absorbed the lesson that sometimes inconsistencies or changes in material culture correlates could signal changing strategies of identification. For example, on Sardinia, the symbolism of the Bronze Age stone towers known as nuraghi has evolved across the millennia in response to social changes (Blake 1998).

A third critique was aimed at the very premise of identity theory. Proponents of social network analysis assert that your connections – whom you know – may be a more important determinant of your behavior than who you are. This shift in emphasis is not a wholesale rejection of identity, however, as network analysts acknowledge that the people who interact have a tendency to already share common attributes, demonstrated in a famous network study of doctors' patterns of prescribing particular drugs (McPherson et al. 2001). Social network analyses can help explain why groups exist and thus reinforce identity studies. In Final Bronze Age Italy, the regions where exotic objects circulated locally, charted as dense ties, developed robust ethnic identities later, while those where exotica did not circulate in any locally preferential way, that is, regions exhibiting few and weak ties, did not form ethnicities (Blake 2014). This seemed to show that close interactions encourage common identities to form, rather than the reverse, homophily. In Bronze Age Italy, the ties are visible before any archaeologically visible collective self-expression. In her 2014 study of the spread of the cult of Jupiter Dolichenus from the Near East to Europe, Anna Collar demonstrated that its spread through the army was not due to soldiers emulating each other out of a sense of common identity, but to the connections afforded by the links between army camps – the interactions made possible the exposure to the cult and its eventual uptake. Network studies have even added nuance to the terminology of identity itself: Matthew Peeples, studying the precontact US southwest, introduced a distinction between categorical and relational identities based on types of networked interactions (2018).

More pointed critiques questioned if identity really did explain human behavior at all in the past. Just because "the pervasive need to construct and reaffirm personal identity is a prevailing theme of post-modern culture" (Dobres and Robb 2000: 13), does not mean this was true in the past. As Brück asserts in her chapter in the Insoll (2007) reader, some actions simply are not identity-driven. The contemporary western obsession with identity need not project back into the past, and ethnographic research suggests that individual self-expression is of truly minimal importance in traditional cultures (e.g. Strathern 1988).

Archaeologists who study hunter-gatherers rarely settle on identity as an explanation for anything they observe in the material record: subsistence strategies, mobility, group size, and structure, all seem best explained in behavioral ecology terms, where environmental pressures shape human responses. Even the art produced in the European caves of the Upper Paleolithic, seemingly symbolic behavior unnecessary for survival, is not immune from these rather functionalist explanations: the scenes may impart information about the annual cycle of animal reproduction, to apparently assist hunters (Bacon et al. 2023). These approaches may be missing something, as Politis and Saunders (2002) show in their ethnoarchaeological study of Amazonian foragers' food taboos. Nonetheless, we must concede that while identity could also be at work in traditional societies, it need not be dominant.

From that perspective, Insoll's claim that scholars of archaeological identity try to "recover an insight into the generation of self at a variety of levels" (2007: 14) seems frankly problematic as an endeavor. As Tarlow (2007: 130) notes,

> Although post-modern concepts of identities as fluid and contingent are philosophically sophisticated, the whole emphasis on identity in social archaeology nevertheless reflects an individualistic, late modern mindset; and the particular fashion for the archaeological diagnosis of the assertion of queer identities, working class identities, ethnic minority identities, identity as resistance and so on, risks underplaying the significance of cultural values, tradition, meanings, belief, economy and the other factors that inform historical relationships and practices. What if ways of doing things in the past were, and are, sometimes not about the expression of identity at all? What if people did things because of values, aspirations, histories and ideas that are not the strategic enactment of identity?

Tarlow (2007) argues that the most successful identity studies have been not the ones that attempt to decipher identities in the past but instead the ones that turn the lens on archaeologists themselves to examine how modern identity politics affect their work – their interpretations of the past, and who gets to do the interpreting. Some of the early feminist studies in archaeology focused on this (e.g. Kramer and Stark 1994), and it remains a vibrant subfield of archaeology that thrives independently of the studies of past identity. Most recently, the elitist nature of the training and the exclusivity of admission to academic archaeology have been the subjects of scrutiny (Heath-Stout 2020). Studies of neo-colonialist and nationalist strands in archaeology (Meskell 2002; Hamilakis 2007; Greenberg and Hamilakis 2022) highlight archaeology's prioritization of the past over present-day inhabitants. This prioritization occurs both physically in such gestures as the razing of neighborhoods to reveal ancient ruins, and ideologically, in the selective erasure of some histories in the purification of the past (see Greenberg and Hamilakis 2022 on instances of this in Greece and Israel). Partly in response to a long history of archaeological colonialism and now neocolonialism, indigenous voices have been amplified in academia in recent decades to reclaim their own heritage and material record (Atalay 2012). In Europe, national archaeological heritage can be problematic when coupled with the sort of primordialist notion of ethnic identity discussed above. The "bitter custody fight" between Austria and Italy (Stone 2000) over Ötzi's remains stalled research on him for many years, until a careful measurement of his findspot placed him 93 m inside Italy. It hardly needs saying that this national boundary had no relevance 5,500 years ago! Movements to implement ethical archaeological practices and to interrogate (academic) archaeology's elite membership continue largely independently of the search for past identities.

These critiques brought nuance to the study of identity without weakening it, at most chipping away at the edges. It took entirely new theoretical approaches beginning in the early 2000s to eventually supplant identity as a subject of interest in archaeological theory circles. The process occurred in parallel with identity's peak in the archaeological literature, so the transition is a fuzzy one. As early as 2005 the edited volume *The Archaeology of Plural and Changing Identities* (Casella and Fowler, eds.) already contained two chapters (by Brück and Fowler) applying the new theories. In 2011, identity was still strong enough for an entire edited volume (Amundsen-Meyer et al. 2011; despite its title, *Identity Crisis*, it was in no way a critique) and for quotes like the following, from Andrew Gardner (2011: 12), "I would therefore go so far as to make the suggestion that all archaeology is ultimately archaeology of and for identity, and that there is no more pressing matter of theoretical and methodological signifi-cance in our discipline [. . .]." We can mark 2018 as something of a *terminus ante quem* for identity in archaeological theory circles when Eva Mol, review-ing Russell et al.'s edited volume on identity published in 2016, starts off with: "This volume offers a series of 12 chapters all (re)addressing a theme that has not been the direct topic of debate for a while [. . .]" (Mol 2018: 723). Among theorists, the entire enterprise of identity work had come to be perceived as hopelessly anachronistic and eurocentric. Yet outside the world of theory, identity studies were expanding. This contradictory dynamic is the subject of the next section.

2 Identity Pushes and Pulls

Since the early aughts, identity studies in archaeology have been subject to conflicting pressures: new theoretical approaches reject identity as a subject of study while new scientific techniques make identity ever more central to the archaeological endeavor. This section explores these competing trends and their impact. For anthropological archaeology, this push and pull brings into sharp relief significant cleavages in the field.

2.1 The Push: Posthumanism and the Threat to Identity Studies

The theoretical approaches attempting to unseat identity studies reject earlier notions of contained human identities altogether. These varied approaches, collectively called "posthumanist," emerged from materiality studies, which had been percolating from the 1990s in archaeology-adjacent fields (Keane 2003). The concept of materiality offered an expanded consideration of how objects influenced and interacted with people, breaking down the perceived distinctions between people, things, and ideas.

Object-oriented approaches foregrounded the material world as active and dynamic in and of itself. Although materiality studies emerged outside archaeology, this was certainly something in our wheelhouse! So, for example, Ötzi's gear made possible (afforded, to use a favored materiality term) his voyage high into the Alps. Moreover, it is imbricated in how we conceptualize him now – archaeologists learned much from his body, but his gear and clothing have done just as much to define him: For example, his bow and arrows and bird belt, the combination of domestic and wild animal hides making up his clothing, even the einkorn wheat and ibex in his gut all *make* him a hunter and an agricultural-ist. There is a correspondence between his possessions and himself, for him and for us.

Materiality studies on their own, initially, could have been absorbed into identity studies as many other theoretical approaches had been, since they both drew to some extent on Bourdieu's agency theory and the early emphasis was on material culture as additive to our pictures of social life, literally the "bundling" that Keane (2003: 414) describes. As Meskell (2008: 3) put it, "This material habitus or lifeworld is a compelling notion: An enmeshing that combines persons, objects, deities, and all manner of immaterial things together in ways that cannot easily be disentangled or separated taxonomically." Meskell (2008: 8) goes on to note materiality's power in identity politics.

But ultimately there was no scholarly appetite for subsuming materiality to the interests of identity studies. Instead, inspired by Latour's (2005) Actor-Network-Theory among others, the new materialists pulled away from identity, not towards it, dismissing any endeavor to determine who people were in the past as the wrong question, and problematizing archaeologists' standard practice of using material culture to make social inferences. To quote Olsen et al. (2012: 203): Meaning has always been confused with representative, symbolic, or metaphorical meaning, whereby the only possible significant role of things is to serve as a window onto cultural or cognitive realms; to provide a means by which to reach something else, something more important. [...] The significance of a boat, for example, is not primarily a function of the symbolic role it potentially may serve [...] *by communicating individual or group identity.* (my emphasis).

For the new materialists, then, the archaeological identity project is flawed, and people should not be the central focus at all. These and other posthumanist approaches reject the primacy of human beings as a legacy of Enlightenment thinking that frames what it is to be human narrowly in a particular type of privileged white male. More than that, they reject taxonomies that divide the material from the ideational, cultural from natural, and symbol from representation. For posthumanists, the best way to interrogate our anthropocentric biases is to change focus. In archaeological posthumanism's most extreme incarnation, symmetrical archaeology, the material world has parity with humans and nonhumans (Olsen 2007). As a consequence, since identity is built on categories – types of humans and human characteristics – and the new focus is far broader than any particular human and their features, identity is rendered irrelevant.

Certainly not everyone in archaeological theory circles abandoned identity: One could grant objects agency, or, better, affect (Crellin and Harris 2021), and still study human identity. Two of the editors of a 2016 volume attempting to bridge these theoretical approaches suggested just that: "The study of material culture is increasingly about memory, experience and affect rather than AngloSaxons, barrow-builders or elites. But the move away from historicising categories to 'worlds' in an ontological sense [...] is not so much a paradigm shift away from identity [...] but rather the growth of a new way to conceptualise it through prioritising materials and material culture" (Maldonado and Russell 2016: 4). The authors frame the new theories as the "third wave of identity," but the reality is that identity had already slipped from use in archaeological theory circles.

2.1.1 The Ontological Turn

Formulations of posthumanism are ontological, meaning that the studies concern states of being, or reality. Ontological studies may be contrasted with epistemological studies, focused on knowledge. Ontological archaeology substitutes for traditional identity a notion of relational personhood, whereby humans are imbricated in relationships with nonhuman things such as animals and inanimate objects, spirits, places, and all are granted personhood (Fowler 2004). Moreover, a human being is not an intact whole, but something both fragmentable (partible) and porous, dividual rather than individual (Harrison-Buck and Hendon (2018: 9). Identity need not reside in a single individual, or even in humans at all. Instead of giving primacy to a solipsistic construction of self, relational ontologies emphasize interactions and the formation of unstable combinations of humans, objects, animals, etc., variously called meshworks (Ingold 2007), bundles (Keane 2003), or assemblages (Deleuze and Guattari 1987; Jones and Hamilakis 2017). Initially in archaeology, personhood was not antithetical to identity; rather, at least according to Fowler (2010), it was one more feature of identity, like gender or age, to be studied. Fowler's (2010: 385) description of the workings of personhood sounds much like identity: "Studies of personhood appreciate that there are different ways that objectification and personification occur, and different ways that people actively and consciously mobilize the materials of the world, including their own bodies, in making themselves and making other people." The theory has evolved away from this position in the past few years, drawing sharper boundary lines between identity and personhood.

There are plenty of examples of apparent relational personhood in European prehistory, but their absence from historical contexts is telling. As Fowler (2010: 379–80) notes: "One reason why personhood has featured more heavily as an area of study in prehistory than history may be that scholars have felt less inclined to focus on how personhood is itself culturally constructed when there are texts written by individuals about their lives and those of others which allow studies of individual biography to be brought to the fore." Fowler's observation is somewhat damning: It is difficult to label someone, a named person, a partible "dividual" if they themselves express a strong sense of being a bounded self.

In prehistory, however, this work is easier. At Dolní Věstonice, evidence abounds for a relational personhood of humans and animals. Human partibility is in a very literal sense evident, with disarticulated human remains intentionally scattered through the settlement layers at Dolní Věstonice and neighboring Pavlov (another Gravettian period site). These remains consist of bones from arms, hands (both isolated bones and bones from the right and left hands of the same individual, perhaps buried with ochre) and feet, as well as teeth (Trinkaus et al. 2010: 664). Furthermore, the intimate co-presence of animal and human bones in formal burials in the Gravettian, discussed below, strongly suggests the personhood of animals.

Moving forward in time, to the Neolithic and later prehistory, the treatment and representations of bodies suggest both that individual bodies were not considered intact solitary entities and that humans could merge identities with animals and objects and be linked to each other through "enchainment" (Chapman 2000; c.f. Jones 2012). These sorts of behaviors are evident across prehistoric Europe. In the Scandinavian Iron Age and Viking era, crania of humans were on occasion detached, curated, and deposited in domestic contexts as objects after death (Eriksen 2020). Animal crania and mandibles were also handled in distinct ways, including placement with and on human bodies (Eriksen 2020: 110). In the seventh and sixth centuries BCE at the indigenous cemetery of Butera, in Sicily, complex mortuary behaviors entailed, variously, deposition of cremated body parts with unburned heads in large jars; parts from multiple individuals buried together; bodies without heads and heads without bodies, and burial jars arranged on top and next to each other in complex configurations (see Adamesteanu 1958 (excavations); Hoernes 2022 for recent discussion). While some of the details elude us because the site was excavated before the advent of bioarchaeology, the general picture is a complex one, and to study Butera in terms of bounded individual identities is to miss the point.

Many of these approaches draw on indigenous ontologies, nonWestern conceptualizations of ways of being that make no rigid distinctions between human, animal, and material worlds. Recognizing that these differences in how the world is perceived may have existed in the past has implications for how we interpret the material, faunal, botanical, environmental, and bioarchaeological records we study. As a measure of the accuracy of our identity labels is how well they align with the lived experience of the people being labeled, this ontological question is a pressing one. These theories are not new in Cultural Anthropology: Strathern in her 1988 book *The Gender of the Gift* described Melanesian conceptions of the partibility of peoples, and their formation in relation to others in contrast to the bounded solitary individual of modern Western culture. Moore's *A Passion for Difference: Essays in Anthropology and Gender* (1994) questioned the ontological primacy of the individual, but it took time for these ideas to take hold in Archaeology.

Alberti (2016: 171) sees much ontological work as not going far enough, with archaeologists essentially mining the ethnographic record for examples of different ways of being that can then be applied to archaeological contexts: "This work aims to reconstruct past ontologies analogously to the reconstruction of past culture. As such, it satisfies our historical curiosities about how other people might have lived quite different lives, building toward a taxonomy of past ontologies." He goes on to say, "such approaches draw their analogies from others' beliefs about reality but do not see these as challenges to the nature of material reality per se." Ontology becomes no more than another word for culture at that point, and we can study other people's ontologies without their impinging on ours. The result? "The effect of the conversion of ontological questions into epistemological ones has made other peoples' claims about reality and their ontological commitments appear trivial or wrong" (Alberti 2016: 171). This inability to move beyond our own framework of knowledge, learning rather than being, seems to be a roadblock in the adoption of the "critical ontology" that Alberti and a very few others propose. What does a critical ontology look like? Its radicalness comes through in Alberti's description of Viveiros de Castro's Amazonian perspectivism (1998), which "posits a "multinatural" metaphysics that inverts the culture–nature relation, replacing our multiple cultures and singular nature with multiple natures (worlds) and a singular culture (way of knowing those worlds)." (Alberti 2016: 172). In all this, the identity project, in the sense of using material culture as a representation of past human identities, would seem to have no place in the "extended sociality that includes animals, spirits, and things" (Alberti 2016: 170). In effect, these posthumanist approaches dislodge the centrality of the study of people built into the very name of anthropological archaeology.

Posthumanism is not without its critics. Problems arise when indigenous ontologies are applied more broadly, outside of the communities where they are held, without crediting the specific thinkers and knowledge-systems involved. Todd (2016), focusing on Latour in particular, lambasts the Euro-Western deployment of indigenous ontologies for use in Western academic and intellectual circles. She argues that this is yet another example of the cultural appropriation of indigenous resources for personal gain (see also van Dyke 2021). Moreover, to relinquish identity politics and descendent communities as subjects and focus instead on objects and depersonalized ontologies strikes some as an abandonment of the living peoples most directly affected by archaeological work (see Fowles 2016).

The timing of the ontological, posthuman turn is interesting for another reason. Just as the catastrophic effects of human-caused climate change on ourselves and on nonhuman objects and living creatures kick in, how convenient to adopt a theoretical position that redistributes agency to the nonhuman world. Some claim that posthumanism is an ethical response to the climate crisis. "I see [ontological anthropology] as a response to a conceptual, existential, ethical, and political problem—how to think about human life in a world in which a kind of life and future that is both beyond the human and constitutive of the human is now in jeopardy" (Kohn 2015: 315). It may be a response, but it is hardly a solution. When Western academics take up an intellectual position promoting relational ontology and nonhuman agency, especially if they are purporting to do this on ethical grounds, if they do not immediately pivot to how accepting that can concretely address climate justice, then this ontological turn serves no other purpose than to shift blame.

2.1.2 Identity's Death Has Been Exaggerated . . .

When one immerses oneself in the archaeological theory literature, identity studies indeed seem dead, giving way to the various "turns": Alberti (2016) dizzyingly flags "the descriptive turn," "the ontological turn," "the material turn," and "the animal turn" all in one article. And, it is certainly the case that posthumanism and the ontological turn are flourishing across academia (Zembylas 2017). As archaeologists tend to follow broader academic trends, the question is, in archaeology, are these new theories sticking outside of theory circles? To quantify these apparent shifts, I compiled data on the evolving popularity of two key terms in posthumanism and identity theory, as shorthand for those two camps. I selected six archaeological journals[2] with a high impact factor and a generalist subject matter and then tallied the number of articles in those journals each year that used the terms "social identity" or "personhood" over the past twenty-two years.

The terms themselves were selected for their simplicity and uniform meaning across varied research questions. I could have come up with a whole slew of identity valences, such as gender and caste, but this would have made the results more opaque. On the other hand, just "identity" was too broad. As for personhood, it is a more specific term than social identity, but its careful application has made it a shorthand for posthumanist studies that engage with relational ontologies and materiality, and downplay identity. I kept the searches broad – scanning the entire text as opposed to just titles or keyword searches – in order to include the highest possible number of articles that were doing or acknowledging identity work or posthumanist approaches, as a means of tracking their relevance. Could an article be critiquing the term? Certainly, but just as a citation is a citation regardless of how it is cited, so is the use of these terms, and presumably the volume of citations is sufficient to weaken any scattered critiques.

My hypothesis was that there would be a marked decline in the use of the phrase "social identity" over time, and especially in the past 5–10 years, and that personhood would be on the rise in the same period, essentially supplanting social identity in the archaeological literature. The results are a surprise to anyone who pays attention to archaeological theory: The data reveal that the

[2] *Antiquity, Cambridge Archaeological Journal, European Journal of Archaeology, Journal of Anthropological Archaeology, Journal of Archaeological Research,* and *Oxford Journal of Archaeology.*

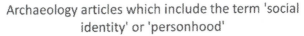

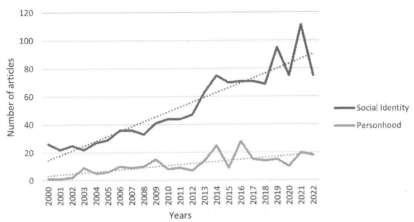

Figure 6 Number of articles using the terms social identity or personhood in six general archaeology journals, 2000–2022. Journals: *Antiquity, Cambridge Archaeological Journal, European Journal of Archaeology, Journal of Anthropological Archaeology, Journal of Archaeological Research*, and *Oxford Journal of Archaeology.*

death of identity studies has been grossly exaggerated (Figure 6). In fact, the opposite is true: Social identity is mentioned more often now than it was ten or twenty years ago. To be sure, there are some ups and downs, but the trendline is one of growth. In contrast, and also surprisingly, "personhood" shows only a modest increase in usage through time. The conclusion to be drawn is that most anthropological archaeologists have not forsaken identity studies in favor of posthumanism.

2.2 The Pull: Advances in Bioarchaeology

If things had gone along much as they had done in the 1960s, 70s, and 80s, with new theories drawing more attention than incremental scientific advances in archaeology, then identity's collapse would have eventually been notable in all corners of the discipline, with only a few old-timers lamenting its loss. But instead, something altogether different occurred. While identity theory was falling out of favor among archaeological theorists, breakthroughs in bioarchaeology were transforming the discipline. In a subfield that began with basic osteological observations, new studies of everything from dental microwear and dental calculus to paleofaeces and microbiomes have opened new avenues of inquiry of human remains. But above all, it is in the fields of archaeogenetics and stable isotope analysis where advances are on such a scale as to warrant calling this the "Third Science Revolution," as Kristian Kristiansen did in the 2014 article credited with being the first full articulation of the phenomenon. Since the 1990s progress in these scientific subfields has proceeded to the point where the quality and quantity of the data being generated have impacted every corner of archaeology. Only in parts of the world where the access to human remains is restricted have these advances been less felt. Although theoretical archaeologists for the most part either disregard the new methods or are actively hostile toward them, the new data being generated are directly relevant to and informative about past identities. Indeed, in anthropological archaeology, bioarchaeological approaches to identity are supplanting material culture as the primary evidence in our analyses.

2.2.1 Archaeogenetic Research: "All the Important Truths"

From the first detection of ancient DNA (aDNA) in the remains of an extinct quagga in 1984, the extraction and sequencing of genetic material from ancient human, animal, and plant taxa have progressed to the point where it is now possible from a range of archaeological contexts, even dirt (Slon et al. 2017). As one might expect, early problems with extraction, contamination, and sequencing of highly fragmented genetic material made archaeologists initially skeptical of the results. Since the 2000s the field has stabilized, and importantly streamlined its methods to make aDNA sequencing available to archaeologists, with enormous consequences. As Higgins et al. (2015: 1) put it, "Advances in DNA analysis of human skeletal remains are providing high-resolution insights into the origin, migrations, health, biogeographic ancestry, phenotype, and identification of deceased individuals and populations," and we can add to this biological sex and kinship. aDNA even determines who is human or not, as the language surrounding Neanderthal and Denisovan DNA exemplifies (Hawks 2013). Identity is at the heart of this data, and aDNA's impact cannot be overstated (see Gokcumen and Frachetti 2020). This is not all for the good: When Crellin and Harris (2020: 38), observe that "DNA is widely understood as a repository of all the important truths about people," they do so with concern for the theoretical weaknesses in archaeogenetic studies.

Nonetheless, examples of how transformative these discoveries are abound. To take gender: The absence of Y chromosomes in the individual in Viking era Grave Bj.581 at Birka, Sweden, recognized as a warrior of high standing, identified them as a biologically sexed female (Hedenstierna-Jonson et al. 2017). This discovery definitively overturned previous assumptions about Norse gender structures and society (Price et al. 2019). In the realm of social structure, aDNA from an individual in the massive Neolithic passage tomb of Newgrange, Ireland, showed they were a child of incest and were also related to other burials in megalithic tombs up to 150 km away. This established that there existed an inherited social hierarchy in Neolithic Ireland, and undermined longstanding theories that egalitarian societies cooperatively built these monuments (Cassidy et al. 2020). But the biggest shockwaves have been felt in studies of migration, and by extension ethnicity. Kristiansen's recent work (2022) describes just how profoundly genetic data are transforming our understanding of population histories and demographic movements. He considers these changes to be as significant to archaeology as the advent of radiocarbon dating in the 1950s, but just as with that earlier revolution, the new data cause "deep anxieties" among some archaeologists (Sykes et al. 2019: 503).

The extraction and sequencing of aDNA are too complex for archaeologists to learn as a side specialization, requiring instead that geneticists be the practitioners. This disciplinary divide has contributed to archaeological skepticism. It didn't help that aDNA seemed to have nothing to do with the instrumentalist notion of ethnicity favored by archaeologists, because archaeogenetics necessarily categorized people exclusively by biological descent. Mirza and Dungworth (1995) fired an early warning shot, voicing concern over the perceived elision of genetic groupings, race, and ethnic groups, equating these genetic studies with long-discredited craniometry. To them, ethnic identity was as problematic as race; they reiterated the identity consensus in noting that ethnicity's seeming fixity and innateness is a mirage, and that ethnic groups are fluid and tactical in their formation, evolution, and dissolution. The article flagged "the potential misuse of DNA research" (p. 351) and then went further, not just critiquing unsound interpretations of DNA data but the whole enterprise: "Research into DNA, and the assumption that DNA can be linked to 'racial' or 'ethnic' groups, is potentially dangerous." (p. 351).

This gatekeeping meant that many archaeologists ignored the developments in archaeogenetic research for several years. Even though I treat archaeogenetics as a subset of bioarchaeology, because indeed it is the extraction of human tissue just as isotope studies is, its practitioners self-identify as geneticists not archaeologists, and are not housed in archaeological departments. So archaeogeneticists beavered away on their own. Despite perennial proposals to collaborate with archaeologists (e.g. Johannsen et al. 2017), archaeogeneticists have tended to integrate archaeological evidence into their data only at the end, as if the data can speak for themselves: The results have been archaeogenetic studies of a descriptive, inductive nature, with sociohistorical questions tacked on (for discussion see Niklasson 2014; Sykes et al. 2019). Archaeologists would not excavate a site and then pose questions later! In rejecting archaeogenetic research, the archaeologists ceded the floor to a scientific community with no training in social theory. But Nobel prizes are to be had (e.g. Svante Pääbo, for sequencing the Neanderthal genome) and this is well funded, highly popular science. The title of prominent archaeogeneticist David Reich's (2018) book *Who We Are and How We Got Here. Ancient DNA and the New Science of the Human Past*, encapsulates just how much ground we archaeologists have lost to the geneticists in studies of past identity.

Frieman and Hoffman (2019) critique archaeogenetics' almost exclusive concern with migration, and a hyper-masculinist take on migration at that. They question "the narrative focus on male conquering warrior hordes, particularly where the implication is that these warriors enjoyed a revered status in society" (2019: 531). They also trouble the assumptions concerning the bounded archaeological cultures (which the public assumes are ethnic groups) on the receiving end of these purported invasions. These extant cultures are labeled "indigenous" simply for being there before the migrants, but since there were numerous waves of settlement and population replacement and admixture, indigeneity is always a relative term. Frieman and Hoffman then critique the bellicose framing of the interactions between the new arrivals and the locals: "This idea of 'protection' from foreign genetic input [. . .] creates a strong analogy of war and threat" (2019: 535). What threat does interbreeding, pose, exactly? Frieman and Hoffman make clear that the nuance has real-world consequences, as this language of genetic invasion has been picked up by the European Alt-right.

The prioritization of aDNA over the material record stems from the perception that because it is biological it is independent of culture, impacting the latter unidirectionally. But as Crellin and Harris note (2020: 44), culture works on DNA, in that we select reproductive partners based on our values, community, status, and so on. They make an impassioned case, drawing on posthumanism, for a rejection of the nature-culture binary that underpins aDNA studies: "Our human body is not just the product of biology, but is shaped by the chairs we sit in, the foods we eat, the world we explore, the air we breathe, the plants that are in our offices, the other people we interact with, the microbes on our skin, and the animals we live alongside. This shaping is in no way simply cultural; it affects our skeletons, our muscles, our brains and indeed our DNA" (2020: 45).

Of course, archaeological resistance to geneticist evidence may also stem from disciplinary rigidity. Using genetic data to identify ancient population groups is no more problematic than using material culture, which is to say, both methods are imperfect but potentially illuminating. Crellin and Harris (2020: 46–47) therefore advocate the kind of mixed-method approach to archaeological data that Uprichard and Dawney (2019) explore for the social sciences.

This involves combining quantitative and qualitative evidence without insistence that they will form a coherent story, rather, accepting the messiness and inconsistencies and not privileging one type of data over another: "Whilst [aDNA] is undoubtedly informative and important it should hold no special status" (Crellin and Harris 2020: 46). They praise smaller scale applications of aDNA, its value in determining biological kinship, for example, where it is integrated necessarily with the archaeological data to form a complete picture of a few people's lives.

Thomas (2006) framed the disconnect between archaeological work and genetic studies as scalar, with archaeologists focused on the local and particular, while geneticists capture continent-wide trends. Semerari et al. (2021) echo this sentiment when noting the difficulties of integrating bioarchaeological data with the cultural identities that are thought to have prevailed in the ancient world. Focusing on the Mediterranean, they observe that the microgroupings we observe archaeologically and historically may be genetically invisible in a Mediterranean-wide DNA. Semerari et al. (2021: 96) recognize that cultural groups will not align in any easy way with bioarchaeological data, because ethnic identities are socially constructed. However, if belonging to a particular cultural group has physical consequences in terms of diet, intermarriage, and so on, the degree of alignment between the biological data and the self-ascription seems important. Semerari et al.'s study demonstrates that aDNA results cannot replace archaeological studies, and they can confirm the constructed nature of cultural identities that theorists have long promoted.

2.2.2 Past Lives and Isotopes

While archaeogenetic research has been exploding, the measurement of stable isotopes in biological tissues has become a mainstay of archaeology in the past few decades, revealing details about the lives of past people that never before seemed knowable. These chemical signatures are generated by diet, climate, and environment, and differences in these factors will be reflected in isotopic ratios, and can thus inform about individual consumption patterns and life histories. Isotope ratios in tissues are datable to the period of tissue formation. Because bones undergo remodeling over a lifespan, isotope values in bones may indicate diet and movement in the past 10–20 years of life, with some variation between bones and based on the individual's age. Isotope values in dental enamel, which don't change after formation in childhood, are particularly useful for getting at origins and at behaviors in the first years of life. In the rare cases of soft tissue preservation, the isotope values of hair may indicate diet in the past few months of a person's life (Szostek et al. 2015: 136–37). While the unit of analysis is the individual, with enough examples, behavioral patterns of groups can be discerned. For all elements the links between the chemical signature in the tissue and the ratio at the source (geologic, faunal, floral, and hydrologic) are not straightforward (Bentley 2006). The complexity of an atom's journey from source to skeleton demonstrates that making inferences from a skeleton's isotope ratios to behavior in the past is a complex business. Stable isotope analysis entered archaeology in the 1970s, with studies of carbon in human bone, and expanded to include strontium (Bentley 2006), oxygen, nitrogen, and sulfur (Nehlich 2015). In the first decades of its application, this geochemical method was applied to questions of economic systems, subsistence, and adaptation, rather than to identity (e.g. Schoeninger and Moore 1992). This has since changed. As there are numerous overviews of stable isotopes and their analysis, what follows is tailored summary of the key isotopes used in identity studies with a few case studies.

Strontium's chemical signature, absorbed into biological tissue through various means (consumption of local flora, fauna, and water) from the surrounding geology, can indicate where a person lived during tissue formation. This has made it critical in discussions of mobility and the composition of communities in prehistoric and historical contexts in Europe. For example, the differences in strontium ratios in Upper Rhine Valley stream water between upland zones and lowland zones allow for inference about people's movements around the area (Bentley 2006: 145–46). However, the meaning of the results may not be straightforward: Bentley (2006: 170) cautions, "Technically speaking, however, a single $^{87}Sr/^{86}Sr$ ratio from enamel does not automatically distinguish a migrant from Place A to Place B from a person who travelled widely throughout childhood." An outlier ratio would indicate mobility, but whether it is the kind experienced by nomadic herders, or due to a single migration event, is not easily answered from the ratios alone. Strontium isotopes can also reveal information about diet. Strontium's decline through biopurification as it moves up the food chain, in comparison to Calcium, means that the Sr/Ca ratio in bones and teeth can reveal trophic levels, that is, the consumer's placement on the food chain, and therefore whether they ate meats or not.

Nitrogen and Carbon isotopes ($\delta^{15}N$ and $\delta^{13}C$) also reveal past diets and by extension, subsistence regimes. Carbon isotope levels indicate the types of plants consumed (C3 or C4, based on the plants' means of photosynthesis). Nitrogen isotopes can indicate the trophic levels of the consumer, and thus clarify whether a high ^{13}C level is due to eating C4 plants, or eating the animals that ate the C4 plants. This combined analysis was put to good effect in Tafuri et al.'s (2009) comparative study of Bronze Age diets in northern Italy and southern Italy, exposing a significant regional difference. The carbon and nitrogen data of humans and animals revealed for the first time that northern Italian people were consuming millet, a C4 domesticate, while southern Italian peoples were apparently relying on wheat and barley, both C3 plants. This recognition of variation in subsistence regimes is a step toward distinguishing regional-level identities.

Oxygen isotope compositions vary by geography and climate, and wind up in a locality in local groundwater or via precipitation (Budd et al. 2004 offer a handy review). Oxygen isotope measurements of dental enamel can indicate place of origin, or at least that an individual is of nonlocal origin even if their actual birthplace is more difficult to determine, since similarly oxygen-enriched groundwater may be present in multiple noncontiguous locations. In those circumstances, historical context is considered. Thus, when early medieval skeletons in Britain have a nonlocal oxygen isotope measurement that fits both with somewhere else in Britain and with parts of Denmark, because of Scandinavian migration the latter explanation has been preferred (Budd et al. 2004).

Beyond the commonly studied isotopes, others are being explored, as are novel combinations of isotopic data. For example, sulfur isotopes, although found in smaller proportions in biological tissues, can be particularly useful in distinguishing diets heavy in freshwater sources from terrestrial diets and show promise in identifying origin also (Nehlich 2015: 11, with examples). Multi-proxy approaches using the data from numerous isotopes are increasingly routine, allowing for more fine-tuned analyses. Analyzing the isotope ratios in enamels of molars that erupt at different stages in childhood exposes variability in diet and residence over short periods in the early years of the person's life. Samples from various tissues can thus reconstruct the life course.

Isotope studies have not met with the same resistance from archaeologists as aDNA. This vastly different reception may be due in part, ironically enough, to identity, in this case, disciplinary identity. Unlike archaeogeneticists, bioarchaeologists conducting isotope research are often in Anthropology departments and there is a culture of engagement with and celebration of social theory that means the field has moved forward in interpretations as the pace of the scientific techniques has advanced. There is even a book series, *Bioarchaeology and Social Theory* (series editor Debra Martin), that is committed to the integration of biological data and culture, and as the series blurb notes, "The interpretations utilize social theory to frame the questions that blend cultural, environmental and social domains so that an integrated picture emerges."

2.2.3 Identity and the Third Scientific Revolution

The transformations in bioarchaeology signal more than just new methods; they are indicative of a changed mindset, in which the human body is treated as an artifact in its own right, at least as important as material culture. Is the explosion in biomolecular studies singlehandedly extending the lifespan of identity studies? To test this I charted the articles using the terms "social identity" and "personhood" in the *Journal of Archaeological Science* and *Journal of Archaeological Science-Reports* (combined here as "science journals") over the past seven years, and compared them with the trendlines of the terms in the general archaeology journals (Figures 7 and 8).[3] The trendlines for "social identity" are remarkably similar by journal type: The science journals are running parallel to general archaeology. "Personhood" is a different case. Far fewer articles include the term overall, and between the two categories of journals defined here, the trendlines are opposing: In general archaeology

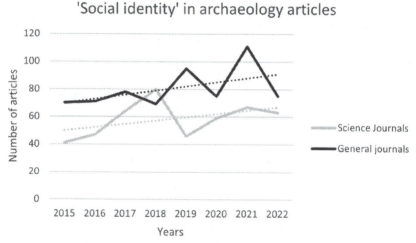

Figure 7 Number of articles using the term social identity in six general archaeology journals and two archaeological science journals, 2015–2022. General archaeology journals: *Antiquity, Cambridge Archaeological Journal, European Journal of Archaeology, Journal of Anthropological Archaeology, Journal of Archaeological Research*, and *Oxford Journal of Archaeology*. Science journals: *Journal of Archaeological Science* and *Journal of Archaeological Science-Reports*.

---

[3] From the foundation of JASR in 2015

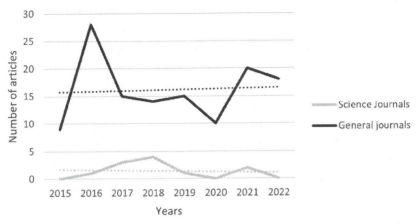

Figure 8 Number of articles using the term personhood in six general archaeology journals and two archaeological science journals, 2015–2022. General archaeology journals: *Antiquity, Cambridge Archaeological Journal, European Journal of Archaeology, Journal of Anthropological Archaeology, Journal of Archaeological Research*, and *Oxford Journal of Archaeology*. Science journals: *Journal of Archaeological Science* and *Journal of Archaeological Science-Reports.*

journals, the term is slightly on the rise since 2015; in archaeological science journals, it is slightly on the decline. Still, the trendlines in both cases are gradual and the data do not suggest that the archaeological sciences are solely responsible for extending the life of a moribund theory.

One may nonetheless interrogate the pattern, asking why theorists shifted away from identity studies just as archaeological scientists came to embrace it in a wholehearted way. Perhaps it did not sit right to have the scientists comfortably apply social theory. In that scenario, statements such as Knudson and Stojanowski's (2008: 398) "we argue that the study of identity is one emerging research theme that is uniquely approachable using bioarchaeological research," may have been nails in the coffin of the identity consensus in archaeological theory circles. To use another metaphor, archaeological theorists may have responded by shifting the goalposts, so that understanding how identities were constructed and negotiated in the past, with which bioarchaeology is ideally suited to help, was no longer a significant problem to solve (see Kuhn 1996: 110). Even if the theorists had no such intentions and the timing is mere coincidence, the general anthropological archaeology community did not follow the theorists in abandoning identity.

3 Bioarchaeology and Identity: Applications

Were adolescents a recognized social group in the Gravettian period? Were the decapitated fellows at the Roman cemetery of Driffield Terrace, York, foreigners or locals? Was Ötzi a vegetarian? Thanks to bioarchaeological data, the answers to these questions of identity are, in order, a cautious yes (Willman 2016), both (Crowder et al. 2020), and no (Dickson et al. 2000). In this section, I examine the application of bioarchaeological studies to several major categories of identity and consider how this work has increased our knowledge of these categories, either by confirming, expanding, or contradicting prior archaeological interpretations. This illustrative rather than exhaustive literature review draws on multiple case studies from mortuary contexts, with Dolní Věstonice II serving as an extended example.

3.1 Kinship

Once a bastion of (hetero)normative archaeological analysis, the study of kinship, a key vector of social identity, has been transformed by an uneasy but exciting combination of cultural anthropological approaches and the new bioarchaeological methods. While archaeologists acknowledge that kinship need not be congruent with biological relatedness, and non-biological descent structures exist and sometimes prevail in some societies, the expectation is the near universality of biological kinship as a structuring factor in collective action among small human groups and traditional societies (see Meyer et al. 2012). In cultural anthropology on the other hand, constructivist approaches to relatedness prevail. Sahlins' (2013: 2) carefully unrestrictive definition of kin as "people who are intrinsic to one another's existence" captures this perspective. In contrast, biological anthropologists have extolled the evolutionary value of biological kin relations for cooperation, altruism, and ultimately group survival (see Johnson and Paul 2016 for an interesting discussion of the disconnects between these two anthropological subfields' diverse perspectives). Archaeologists have been relatively slow to engage with the constructivist approach to kinship. Instead, early applications of bioarchaeology to kinship studies focused on identifying postmarital residence patterns (if exogeny, exogamy, or some other pattern prevailed, for example). Johnson and Paul (2016: 83–84) describe the logic: "The assumption is that the more mobile sex will exhibit greater intrasite skeletal/dental variation, and the non-mobile sex will exhibit greater intersite variation and biodistance." Built into the premise of these studies is biological relatedness of family units with genetic variation only in the marriage partner.

Using both phenotypic and genetic methods,[4] more recent work on kinship makes no such assumption, looking for correlates between burial structures and genetic relationships, whether in an individual tomb ("small grave analysis") or from spatial clustering in cemeteries. Sometimes there is no visible patterning in burial arrangements, and then the genetic evidence can help to reveal relationships. But many times, when archaeologists find burials adjacent to each other, such as those in megalithic mounds or in a corner of a village cemetery, they will hypothesize kin groups and then test to determine genetic relatedness. Sometimes expectations are confirmed. This was the case in the study of a Middle Neolithic chamber tomb at the German site of Benzingerode, where among the jumble of bodies, several close genetic relatives were found lying near or on top of each other (Meyer et al. 2012). Similarly, aDNA of late Neolithic group burials at Eulau, Germany confirmed biological sex and revealed a nuclear family unit in one grouping (Grave 99). Furthermore, strontium isotope data showing nonlocal origins of the adult females at the site suggested apparent patrilocality (Haak et al. 2008).

Sometimes, the aDNA reveals something unexpected. When females are found with babies or children in the same grave, the assumption of maternal–child relations finds near total acceptance. Yet in one startling case, results from an aDNA study of a Neolithic woman (KZ1) and baby (KZ3) double burial and nearby toddler (KZ2) from the Polish site of Krusza Zamkowa showed that none of the three were related to each other on the maternal line (Figure 9; Juras et al. 2017). In other words, the woman was not the mother of either child, nor were the baby and toddler maternal siblings. Back at Eulau, Grave 98 offers another complex case (Haak et al. 2008). There an adult female and three children were grouped together. The youngest child, a baby, was found facing the woman and almost cradled by her. The baby's poor preservation prevented aDNA retrieval. The other two children, who were siblings at least maternally but not related to the woman, were facing her back, a position that does not convey affective ties, at least to our modern eyes. The aDNA could be read as confirming the hypothesis of biological kinship of the two older children and lack thereof with the woman, suggested by the arrangement of the bodies. The aDNA thus does not lead the interpretation, it informs it.

Given these insights, Brück's (2021) critique of bioarchaeological approaches to kinship seems unwarranted. Focusing on Bronze Age Britain, Brück takes issue with a series of recent articles that used aDNA and isotopic evidence to claim that later prehistoric Central European societies were

---

[4] Traditional biodistance methods use comparison of phenotypic traits such as odontometrics and craniometrics to infer kin connection and population groups. aDNA may supplant that work entirely but for the moment both methods are used when possible.

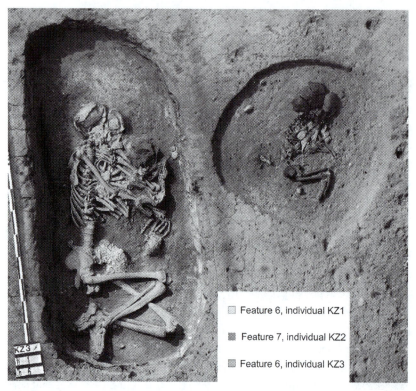

Feature 6, individual KZ1

Feature 7, individual KZ2

Feature 6, individual KZ3

Figure 9 In situ ortophotograph of three individuals (KZ1, KZ2, and KZ3) from Krusza Zamkowa archaeological site, Poland. Reprinted from *Forensic Science International-Genetics*, Vol 26, A. Juras et al., Investigating kinship of Neolithic post-LBK human remains from Krusza Zamkowa, Poland using ancient, pp. 30–39 © (2017), with permission from Elsevier.

patriarchal, structured around monogamous nuclear families and practicing female exogamy. She responds that "the presence of individuals who are paternally related in the cemeteries analysed in those studies does not tell us how those relationships operated or were conceptualised, how they were thought to be created, or whether they represented the only important familial links. Nor indeed can patrilineality be used to infer particular forms of social relationships, between men and women, for example" (2021: 233–34). Brück is correct to call out undertheorized interpretations of the bioarchaeological data on kinship, (as bioarchaeologists themselves are rigorously addressing: see Ensor et al. 2017). Yet her critique goes beyond that: The bioarchaeologists are faulted for ignoring questions that their data simply cannot answer.

In fact, in bioarchaeologically based theorizing, there is reason to be optimistic. Johnson and Paul's (2016) quantitative literature review showed a sharp increase, starting in the 2000s and continuing to rise in the 2010s, in bioarchaeological journal articles that addressed not just biological kinship but biosocial and social kinship as well (Johnson and Paul 2016: Table 4). They also note that while the traditional bioarchaeological studies of genetic relatedness continue, some bioarchaeologists are focusing on non-biological relatedness. Pilloud and Larsen's (2011) phenotypic study of teeth from interments at the Turkish Neolithic settlement of Çatalhöyük is a case in point. At Çatalhöyük, the dead were buried under house floors, sometimes as many as thirty in a single house, added over time. Pilloud and Larsen hypothesized that the dead in the same house would display phenotypic similarities that indicate genetic relatedness, and that at the scale of the city itself, houses with genetically related individuals would be near each other. Neither hypothesis proved to be true. In the abstract the authors state that "These findings suggest that Çatalhöyük may not have been a kin-based society," a problematic claim relying on a biological understanding of kinship. However, at the end of the study, their interpretation of the results is more theoretically nuanced: "Instead, the site may have been organized by an alternate definition of kin that was not defined in terms of genetic relationships. These 'kin' groups could have formed for various social functions creating a more fluid definition of family" (pp. 527–28). This oft-cited article signals a welcome advance in bioarchaeological theory.

Another intriguing case is the triple burial at the Gravettian site of Dolní Věstonice, in Moravia, Czech Republic, introduced earlier. The 31,000-year-old inhumation of three people in their teens had initially been interpreted in ways that resonate in a heteronormative Western society. Importantly, however, with the emergence of more bioarchaeological data, a progressive recalibration is evident. The curious (to modern eyes) arrangement of the bodies elicited speculation from the beginning: The two outer bodies (DV 13 and DV 14) were sexed male from pelvic examination, and the central figure (DV 15) was initially unsexed because of a pelvic pathology. The left male (DV 13) had been arranged with his hand resting on DV 15's pubic area, while the right male (DV 14) was buried face down with his left arm draped over DV 15's right arm. The early report of the 1986 excavations, assuming as would many subsequent publications that the unsexed DV 15 was a female based on the person's gracile build, read the scene as follows: "The arrangement of the grave and the position of the bodies vis-à-vis each other may mirror a real-life drama which precipitated the burials. If, for example, the woman died during unsuccessful childbirth, the two men might have been thought responsible for this and had to involuntarily follow her into the afterlife." (Klíma 1987: 835). That the excavator went immediately to a maternal role for the purported female speaks to engrained stereotypes, as does the androcentric assumption of the men as the agents with the autonomy to be somehow responsible for this woman.

Other bioarchaeological data took analysis of the trio in a new direction. Shared odontological traits of all three individuals made it likely that the three were related (Alt et al. 1997), and then identical mitochondrial DNA from DV 14 and DV 15 indicated shared maternal lineage (Fu et al. 2013). Mittnik et al. (2016) extracted DNA to sex DV 15 and determined that the central individual was chromosomally male. Even before then, however, Svoboda (2006: 22) suggested that the indeterminate gender may have been a feature of the individual's identity in life, and Mittnik et al. (2016: 5/9) themselves note, "The fact that his sex was undeterminable by means of bone morphology and metrics suggests a unique character of this person." In subsequent analyses, the presentation of this data is done with caution, making no inferences about the relationships between the trio beyond DV 14 and DV 15 likely being siblings and, given the odontological traits shared with DV 13, a suggestion that he could have been a paternal relative. The physical closeness of the bodies and the arms of the flanking figures that crossed the central figure suggest a bond, or perhaps the portrayal of a bond by the people arranging the corpses. By knowing that two were siblings and a third was also likely related, along with the depositional arrangement, it may be reasonable to infer a kinship bond between these individuals. This contrasts with the double burial of the same period at Sunghir, Russia, an equally extraordinary Gravettian period site. There, two adolescent males were buried head to head with large quantities of grave goods, including thousands of beads made of mammoth ivory. They were not in fact close relatives (Sikora et al. 2017). Indeed, the genomic data from those burials and other human remains at Sunghir led the researchers to argue for exogamy among these Upper Paleolithic populations. The small sample size and exceptional nature of the burials mitigate against such sweeping claims, but the takeaway is that if kin identities mattered at Sunghir as they did at Dolní Věstonice, it was not a biologically derived kinship. In the studies of these enigmatic sites, the new data have been fundamental in expanding our knowledge and improving our interpretations of kinship in past societies.

3.2 Social Status

While in death as in life, the wealthy and powerful tend to leave behind the most enduring traces and receive the most attention from archaeologists and the public at large, a new interest in revealing non-elites is evident in some high-profile field projects, such as the Old Kingdom workers encampment at Giza

(Lehner 2002) and the Roman Peasant Project (Bowes 2021), and this concern with non-elite lives is the thrust of new work at Pompeii (e.g. Notarian 2023). Bioarchaeology has contributed much new data on social groups but so far, such studies have not proven transformative, instead serving to confirm prior archaeological interpretations of social status. Studies across multiple cultures have demonstrated that dietary variability within a population can often be attributed to social differentiation (see Schutkowski et al. 1999). This is the premise behind much of the work being done, although in fact in reverse: The bioarchaeologists have an a priori understanding of their subjects' social position from the archaeological proxy data, and they insert the dietary data into that existing framework. In the more straightforward cases, of which there are admittedly many, the skeletons in rich burials exhibit different diets from those in modest burials, and by measures of animal protein and diversity of diet, the rich win out. Such is the case for the burials from the Late Halstatt/Early La Tène late fifth century BCE site of Glauberg, Germany. There, the individual buried in Tumulus 1 and equipped with gold, weapons, and other high-value grave goods, had consumed a diet high in meat and C3-plants, while the informally buried individuals placed in conical pits typically used for food storage showed low meat consumption and a diet of C4 plants, almost certainly millet (Knipper et al. 2014). The authors conclude, "The dietary information of the carbon and nitrogen isotope ratios contributes to the difference between the 'prince' and the individuals in the conical pits and the ditches and confirms his outstanding social position" (Knipper et al. 2014: 831). The researchers present other interesting findings, about the catchment area under this local ruler's control based on animal husbandry practices and on the probable place of origin of some of the people in the pits. Thus the bioarchaeological data add a level of detail to the composition and activities of social groups at Glauberg, while confirming the general contours already established by the archaeology.

Studies from elsewhere in Europe make similar contributions. For example, Richards et al.'s (1998) study of $\delta^{15}N$ and $\delta^{13}C$ values from forty-one individuals in the Roman cemetery at Poundbury Camp, England, found a correlation between dietary difference and burial type in the Late Roman period. The people in the fancier graves (mausolea and lead coffins) had a more diverse diet combining marine and terrestrial proteins than the people buried in wooden coffins, who ate little marine protein. The authors began by assuming these burial types denoted higher status, and then inferred that marine protein's absence from the wooden coffin folks' diet was an indicator that seafood was reserved for elites.

Are there cases where a correlation between archaeologically indexed wealth differences and dietary differences is not observed? In Le Huray and

Schutkowski's (2005) isotope analysis from three late La Tène cemeteries in the Czech Republic (as well as graves in Austria), fairly egalitarian burials disguise some apparent differences in diet. The cemeteries themselves exhibit no major hierarchical differences, consisting of uniformly modest inhumations with varied grave goods. However, isotope values of the biologically sexed males buried with weapons differ from that of the rest of the population, including both males without weapons and females. Relatively elevated δ^{15}N levels among the armed males are interpreted as indicating a diet higher in animal protein for the "warriors" than the general population. Interestingly, biologic-ally sexed women buried with torqs and other seemingly valuable grave goods exhibit no differences in isotope values from the women lacking grave goods of value. While the isotopic analysis revealed something we did not already know about these populations, it does not upend the interpretation provided by the material culture: The dietary differentiation reinforces some traditional assump-tions about the social value of warriors in Iron Age Europe. This kind of reinforcement of existing expectations appears to be true in most isotope studies inferring status from diet: The data of individual diet and lifestyle will not easily dislodge the impression of relative status conveyed by a tomb and its grave goods. In the case of the women with the torqs who ate the same diet as women without torqs, the interpretation is that women of all social levels had the same diet, not that the women we thought were high-status were not. Thus, in practice, the archaeological evidence has the upper hand.

Similarly, in a study of the δ^{13}C and δ^{15}N values of seventy-seven individuals from ten sites in the Roman Iron Age (first to fourth centuries CE) Denmark, the diet across social classes was uniformly high in terrestrial proteins (Jørkov et al. 2010). The authors' deference to the archaeological record appears in the very title of the article, "Uniform Diet in a Diverse Society." They propose that the relative homogeneity in isotope ratios across "rich" and "simple" graves could disguise differences in cuts of meat or the preparation of the food, rather than suggesting something more radical, that perhaps burial status was constructed differently from status in life. Nor do Jørkov et al. use the patterning to qualitatively assess what it meant to belong to a particular class in this society.

One study that breaks with this deference to the archaeological and historical record is Vidal-Ronchas et al. (2019). In this study of the δ^{13}C, δ^{15}N, and δ^{18}O values of bones and enamel from forty-four individuals from Late Avar Period (680–822 CE) graves in Nuštar Croatia, the authors observe dietary homogeneity in the midst of clear wealth divisions between graves. Vidal-Ronchas et al. (2019: 1727) prioritize the dietary data, affirming that "Diet is often an accurate proxy for social status, especially in Europe, where food has been extensively linked to social roles." The authors do suggest that the homogeneous isotopic data cannot capture potential differences in quality and cuts of meat, but mostly they attempt to fit the isotopic pattern they observe into a larger "social homogenization" process across the region in the Late Avar period. Why the graves are still clearly differentiated (e.g. two individuals were each buried with a horse, a high-status item if ever there was one) is not explained.

In addition to isotopic studies of diet, bioarchaeological studies of skeletal traumas, traces of malnutrition, and parasites contribute to a picture of the experiences of social groups. A study of 275 individuals from an eleventh to twelfth centuries CE cemetery in Giecz, Poland, revealed high rates of stress-related skeletal traumas (evident in 49% of individuals) that the authors attribute to a life of extreme hard work that began in childhood (Agnew and Justus 2014). They stop short of using the bioarchaeological data to make inferences about the social categorization of the individuals under study, due to uncertainty about the representativeness of their sample: "Since the cemetery excavation remains incomplete, it is unknown if the Giecz Collection is truly representative of the living population in medieval Giecz. However, all ages and both sexes are well represented across the sample, suggesting that the cemetery site Gz4 contains those comprising a normal population and not one restricted to only certain sectors (e.g. military troops, clergymen, etc.)." The reluctance to use the compelling osteological data to infer social divisions in the absence of more contextual evidence highlights the deference described above.

However, archaeogenetic data can reveal information about social structure we would not know otherwise: Mittnik et al.'s (2019) study of Early Bronze Age household cemeteries in southern Germany discovered that the differences evident in the wealth value of graves played out in genetic relatedness as well: The wealthy graves clustered together constituted biological families, while the poorer graves in proximity to each wealthy cluster were of unrelated although local individuals. The authors inferred that this was evidence of hierarchy within households composed of affluent families with enslaved servants. Organized multigenerational enslavement in rural households in this period was a surprise, transforming our understanding of the structure of Early Bronze Age society in Europe.

Thus, while bioarchaeological data contributes to the reconstruction of social structure in the past, many of these studies do not call into question, in a manner that is true for other valences of identity, individuals' actual status. A healthy well-nourished person from a modest grave will indicate that non-elites enjoyed a healthy lifestyle, not that the individual was in fact elite. Yet Parker Pearson's seminal 1982 study demonstrated that ideology interferes with the straight representation of lived status differences in burials. Even when the bioarchaeological data align with the archaeological data, there is more to be said. What would having the diet indicated by the isotope data have meant to the residents? It seems, for example, that it would have been better to be a non-elite in Poundbury Camp, Britain in the Roman period than in Glauberg Germany in the La Tène period. Thus, the addition of bioarchaeological data provides much needed detail but has rarely overturned inferences of social status in past societies.

3.3 Age

Calculating age-at-death, one of the labors of the osteologist, continues to be methodologically challenging especially when studying older adult skeletons (Knudson and Stojanowski 2008: 402–403). Age studies are interpretatively complex as biological age and social age need not align and will be influenced by the individual's other identity valences. Nonetheless, progress has been made; different strontium signals in tooth enamel and in bone have been used to discuss patterns of mobility and migration over a person's life. Combined with dietary questions, this variation between bones and teeth also reveals something about children's experiences, their nutrition compared to adults, and weaning practices. Indeed, the tissue regeneration varies from bone to bone, so isotope ratios taken from multiple bones could capture where the person was and what they ate at different stages of their life, through adulthood. This was done with Ötzi, whose $\delta^{18}O$ values on tooth enamel combined with strontium and lead isotopes point to a childhood home in the Eisack Valley, while the oxygen isotope values of his bones indicated movement in adulthood to other Alpine regions over the decades, although the total range was only about 60 km from his findspot (Müller et al. 2003).

Pearson and Meskell (2015): 472 fuse isotopic evidence and theories of the body and age and gender at Çatalhöyük to argue for a status conferred in maturity that was more pronounced than gender differences. They conclude, "In sum, the isotope analysis with the skeletal and burial data suggests that age rather than gender was the primary axis of difference. The mean isotope ratios for carbon and nitrogen for females and males is virtually identical (Pearson 2013), strongly suggesting that they had similar diets."

New work on adolescence is similarly benefiting from expanded bioarchaeological data. Adolescence is both a biological and cultural phenomenon. As French and Nowell (2022: 2) put it, " … social definitions of the length and duration of adolescence are both more variable than those based on biological markers, and in turn, may actually influence the timing and duration of biological adolescence." Nonetheless, that the onset of puberty and related biological development at 10–24 years of age is broadly uniform across human species through time provides a baseline for examining the cultural construction of adolescence in various societies. Dolní Věstonice is again a useful reference, showing the value of bioarchaeology in decentering modern Western norms. Soon after discovery, the individuals were typically characterized in the literature as "young people" or "young individuals" (e.g. Klima 1987; Formicola et al. 2001: 372) although we have no idea whether that relative descriptor had meaning in the Upper Paleolithic. In the later literature, however, the term "young" does not appear, just the raw age estimates are given (DV 13: 17-19 y.o.; DV 14: 16-17 y.o.; and DV 15: 20 y.o. (Mittnik et al. 2016: 2)). Data from a surprising source – dental wear from DV 13, 14, and 15 – may hint at coming-of-age rituals. DV13, 14, and 15 all exhibit wear on the cheek (buccal) side of the canine and postcanine teeth. While on DV13 and 15 this wear appears bilaterally, DV 14, who is estimated to be an adolescent and thus slightly younger than the other two, shows wear on only one side of his mouth. Such wear has been documented elsewhere as being caused by cheek plugs or labrets, and Willman (2016) hypothesizes that facial piercings may have been added during a rite of passage, one earlier rite, and then another later (postadolescence) (see also Frayer et al. 2020). Not everyone accepts this: French and Nowell (2022) argue that there were no clear age-related distinctions in burial practices in the European Upper Paleolithic, from which they infer that in these communities adolescents were not recognized as a distinct category from adults. They did not engage with Willman's theory in their own discussion. The theory is nonetheless compelling for suggesting age-based social groupings. Further examples may resolve this with the molecular methods now at our disposal.

3.4 Animals and Identity

In a growing area of research, occupational identities and human–animal relationships are made more accessible through isotope analysis of domesticated animals (e.g. Müldner et al. 2014). Although the significance of the diet and mobility of domesticates may be framed in the economic language of exploitation and land use, the data are also applied to reconstructions of the occupational identities of herders and their lifeways. Sjögren and Price (2013) assessed the mobility of domesticates based on strontium and oxygen isotope data from thirty-nine animal teeth from two Neolithic settlements in Falbygden, Sweden. They argued that the circulation of animals (particularly cattle) across western Sweden in the Neolithic Funnel Beaker (TRB) period may explain the shared ritual practices evident in the farflung megalithic monuments in the region. In other words, the commonalities in ritual practices arose in a context of complex regional social networks that the cattle's mobility reflects. The authors draw on an earlier isotopic study of human remains from several passage graves which showed that 25% of the burials had nonlocal origins (Sjögren et al., 2009, cited in Sjögren and Price 2013: 691). The cattle capture even more this mobility: 60% of the twenty-one cattle teeth tested were arguably or securely nonlocal. The isotope values of the nonlocal cattle were not homogeneous, meaning that there was no single source for the animals, and instead perhaps a region-wide network. In contrast, the isotope values of pigs were almost all local, while the sheep were a mix of local and nonlocal.

Domesticates need not be the only subjects of such studies. In the Gravettian, animals were intricately connected to human lives, suggesting an ontology of personhood for animals. Animal bones are found intentionally and intimately mixed with human burials. At Dolní Věstonice II, besides the perforated carnivore (fox and wolf) teeth found with all three skeletons, the individual DV 15 had a charred reindeer pelvis bone in their mouth (Klima 1987: 834; Svoboda 2006: 21; French and Nowell 2022: 9 initially described it as a horse rib). Klima at the time of excavation suggested this may have been a "biting device used to overcome pain" given the individual's serious infirmities. In light of the extensive supporting evidence for animal roles in Middle Upper Paleolithic society, including the distributions of animal bones, especially mammoth, at Gravettian settlements and burials, and a predominantly zoomorphic artistic repertoire, the bone in DV 15's mouth may have served as more than just a tool. A biomolecular study of the animals whose remains are found at Gravettian burials may illuminate further these human–animal relationships: for example, sex selection, age-at-death, and genetic relationships. Thus, bioarchaeological data on animal life histories can inform on economic systems, but also ideology, regional scale identities, religious practices, and human–animal relationships.

3.5 Pathologies, Nonnormative Categories, and Social Values

How societies treat individuals with visible pathologies offers insights into identity construction, disease culture, and social values. The delimiting of the boundaries of normative social identities is a subject of study to which bioarchaeological data can contribute. Some bioarchaeologists approach this through the framework of queer theory. As Hollimon (2017: 55) puts it, "'queer' is by definition what is at odds with the normalized, the legitimated, or the dominant." This framework offers numerous entry points into deviance and nonnormative identities in the archaeological record, but here we will focus on pathologies. While osteological study has long recorded pathologies that could have led to deviant status in life and triggered nonnormative burial practices, these studies have advanced with the advent of better techniques on the one hand, and more sophisticated theorizing on the other. The result is an exploration of *disease culture*, "which contextualizes paleopathological data in the culturally specific views of the disease" (Knudson and Stojanowski 2008: 408). The terms themselves convey the complexity of today's bioarch-aeological approaches to disease: "Bioarchaeologists are increasingly distin-guishing between *disease*, which is a temporary or permanent pathological condition, *impairment*, the physical or mental state that may result from a disease, and *disability*, which is the relationship between society and individuals with impairments" (Knudson and Stojanowski 2008: 409).

Distinctions between volitional and non-volitional social deviance need not have obtained in the past (Shay 1985), so we may expect individuals with pathologies to receive distinct mortuary treatment. This seems to have been the case in the Middle Upper Paleolithic. French and Nowell (2022) record pathologies or abnormalities in 36 percent of the Middle Upper Paleolithic adolescents they studied, an extraordinarily high number given the current global rate of congenital abnormalities in newborns of 6 percent (Lobo and Zhaurova 2008). Back at Dolní Věstonice, DV 15's skeleton revealed extensive pathologies including scoliosis and bowed longbones (Formicola et al. 2001), the authors remarking on the elaborate funerary ritual for an otherly abled individual. Combined with other examples from the Gravettian period in Europe, Formicola et al. (2001: 378) comment "Rich ornamentation, elaborate funerary behavior, and site of inhumation shed light on ideological aspects, strengthening the idea that a few Upper Paleolithic burials included selected individuals and that physical diversity may have played a role in selective burial patterns from that period." Although not intended to be discriminatory, the interpretation can be read as an attempt to ascribe to disparate individuals with varied pathologies a membership in a single group. Whether one perceives the approach as empowering for otherly abled people, or a form of othering, the data moved our knowledge forward.

Without conflating the disparate life experiences of these diverse individuals, we can at least infer that their societies responded similarly to the middle individual – DV15 – at Dolní Věstonice, the child (Sunghir 3) in the Sunghir burials, and to the adolescent skeleton exhibiting dwarfism in the later Epigravettian burial at Romito Cave Italy (Formicola 2007). The overrepresen-tation in the death of these individuals suggests that otherly abled people were buried in an archaeologically visible way to a higher degree than the general population. Were these individuals revered or punished for their conditions?

DV 15 was not apparently shielded from work. Skeletal hypertrophy in DV 15's lower limbs speaks to an active, even strenuous life; this "probably reflects both mobility (local or long distance) and burden carrying" despite the pathologies (Trinkaus et al. 2001: 1292). Furthermore, their teeth show the same traces of wear that their grave mates exhibit: Distinctive striations on the front teeth that suggest all three engaged in work involving their teeth, perhaps in the scraping of hides. They may have held the hide in their teeth and pulled it taut with one hand while scraping it with a tool in the other hand. The tool sometimes hitting the teeth would lead to the cutmarks (Willman 2016). Were the individuals in the Gravettian burials sacrificed, as Formicola (2007) suggests, together with one or more family members? We cannot say, but the multiple burials may exemplify the porosity of personhood. The bioarchaeological documentation of pathologies and their frequency importantly calls into question any claims to social hierarchies in the Gravettian. As Graeber and Wengrow (2021: 104) note, "the idea that these tombs mark the emergence of some sort of hereditary aristocracy seems the least likely of all [interpretations]. Those interred were extraordinary, 'extreme' individuals. Anomalous in almost every respect, such burials can hardly be interpreted as proxies for social structure among the living." It is the bioarchaeological evidence that pushes our understanding of these people, and their place in their communities, beyond a notional elite.

The malarial infants buried in the ruins of an Italian villa in the Late Roman period are another case where paleopathological analysis can provide an explanation for abnormal burial and disease culture in this community (Soren et al. 1995). At Poggio Gramignano, Umbria, the forty-seven young victims were buried in haste but with care, the babies swaddled, with occasional, possibly apotropaic, tokens, and some slaughtered puppies (Wilson 2022). The evidence conveys the fear and grief gripping the community at a time when the cause of these premature deaths was not known, and when witchcraft was the best response.

Bioarchaeological data – in particular isotopic analysis – has been critical to the interpretation of the Roman cemetery at Driffield Terrace, York, where more than half of the seventy-five interred individuals had been decapitated, and some were buried prone (Müldner et al. 2011). What triggered this treatment? Because they are all male except for one sexed female, it has been suggested that the cemetery was for soldiers, or gladiators (Müldner et al. 2011: 280). High rates of antemortem skeletal trauma point to active lives involving accidents and interpersonal violence (House et al. 2012), although whether the decapitation was a form of execution or occurred postmortem in a Romano-British burial ritual is a matter of debate (Crowder et al. 2020: 4). Multi-isotope analysis of the strontium, oxygen, carbon, and nitrogen values in dental enamel and bone collagen of the deceased revealed several individuals with origins outside

Britain (possibly from Transylvania). Furthermore, there was more diversity overall in the isotope values than one finds in the more typical cemeteries around York. However, most of the dead in the cemetery were likely from Britain and, specifically, quite local (Crowder et al. 2020). This analysis determined that there was no evident correlation between place of origin and burial rite, that is, cultural identity was not the axis of difference triggering this differential treatment.

3.6 Sex and Gender

Bioarchaeological studies are making important contributions to the reconstruction of gender systems in the past. This work began in a conventional fashion, ascribing gender from the binarized sexing of the skeleton, and then comparing the lifestyles of individuals by gender, such as health and diet, mobility, division of labor, violence, and age-at-death. Differences in $^{87}Sr/\,^{86}Sr$ ratios in dental enamel along gender lines, when indicative of residency in early childhood, have been used to infer matrilocal or patrilocal societies (Bentley 2006: 175). The bioarchaeological study of the early medieval cemetery in Giecz Poland mentioned in 3.2 revealed that rates of skeletal traumas caused by occupational stress, and where on the body they occurred, were not statistically different between men and women. Thus, no clear gendered division of labor was revealed; whatever the specific tasks were, the work was equally strenuous for all (Agnew and Justus 2014). Isotope analysis has been particularly fruitful in identifying gendered dietary differences within populations, especially emphasized with the transition to farming. It has been difficult to separate physiological conditions from nutritional ones. Isotope data are helping to settle the debate. For example, across a range of early Neolithic (Linearbandkeramik) sites in Europe, males consistently had the same or slightly higher $\delta^{15}N$ values than females, suggesting that some males ate a little more meat (Hedges et al. 2013: 355). This sort of study does not call into question gender constructions themselves, but it does add to the picture of gendered lifeways.

If bioarchaeology began with a rather conventional approach to gender, that has changed. Starting with Sofaer's (2006) work on the socially constructed body, there are now plenty of bioarchaeologists who, as Agarwal (2012: 323) puts it, "are keenly interested in engagement with social theory." Hollimon (2017) details case studies of the recognition of nonbinary individuals through bioarchaeology, noting that when occupational specialization is gendered, the osteobiographical analysis of individual graves may reveal slippages between sex and gender. This is not always easy to interpret. While bioarchaeologists are adept at interrogating the social construction of gendered difference as separate from a baseline of binarized biological sex, it has proven much more challenging to treat the baseline itself, sex, as both biological and cultural. Some pushback is evident: Masclans Latorre et al. (2021: 233) oppose dissolving the baseline, insisting, "We need a language to discuss the categories created by skeletal, and increasingly aDNA, analysis." They decide, "Therefore, 'gender' will be used hereinafter to refer to the cultural attributes and 'sex' to the predominant biological differences, as a starting point from which to determine how strongly the latter is expressed in the former." If this sounds like a retreat, it need not be: The authors are open to slippage in the construction of both, without foregoing the terms altogether.

The contributors to the edited volume of Agarwal and Wesp (2017), *Exploring Sex and Gender in Bioarchaeology*, each demonstrate the compatibility of gender theory with scientific analyses of human remains. As Rosemary Joyce (2017: 2) notes in her discussion piece in the volume, "What contradicts an assumption that feminist archaeologists like me might have been tempted to make – that bioarchaeology would automatically universalize modern sexed ideologies – is the realist orientation of bioarchaeology, which begins with methodological engagement in a close examination of skeletal remains. Bioarchaeologists are witnesses to the actual existence of less certainty and less dualism than the folk model that grounds the Western dichotomous gender system in two natural sexes." This is critical: bioarchaeologists' necessary starting point, the base unit of the individual, ensures that they are always already intersectional in their approach in a way that archaeologists excavating households, for example, cannot be. We saw this with DV 15. Similarly, Sunghir 3 (S3) the smaller skeleton in Grave 2 of another famous Gravettian burial site, Sunghir, was assumed to be female but the genomic evidence revealed male chromosomes (Sikora et al. 2017: 659). When S3 was thought to be a female, differences in grave goods between that individual and adjacent male S2 were parsed along gender lines, so, more ivory spears with S3, but the longest one with S2; alpine fox teeth with S2 but not S3, and so on (Trinkaus et al. 2014: 18–23). Reading the 2014 passage, the difficulties in comparing the grave goods through the lens of binarized gender are evident, and the authors themselves questioned why children would have had all this stuff in the first place. The genetic data change all that: The differences in grave goods may still have something to do with gender, but they are not biologically grounded and could have different meanings entirely (Sikora et al. 2017). This is liberating.

Not everyone agrees. Geller (2017: 86) sounds the alarm about the "geneticization" of gender: "Bioarchaeologists' use of genetic testing to sex juveniles illustrates subtle deterministic notions about social identity with little, if any, regard for socialization, play, parenting, or communal childcare." Agarwal

(2012) questions the bioarchaeological habit of categorizing by biological sex at the beginning of any study of a group, rather than by a different axis of difference, such as urban and rural. This prioritizing of sex renders it difficult to interrogate the importance of that division among all the others that organize individuals. Soriano et al. (2021) tried something different in the first-ever queer theory approach to the Bell Beaker phenomenon in Spain. They were able to argue convincingly for gender fluidity before adulthood, and, importantly, numerous exceptions to the expected binary of male – warrior; female – textile worker. Indeed, their study demonstrated that other categories determined an identity that cross-cut biological sex, and were probably more important, such as age and status. While traditional approaches continue (e.g. Vaňharová and Drozdová's (2008) use of aDNA to sex juvenile skeletons from Beaker burials in Czech Republic) as in all subfields, the vanguard of bioarchaeologists who apply queer theory to their subjects is growing. Hollimon (2017: 57) proposes, "If we view sex as a category of bodies and gender as a category of persons, we can better understand Native North American gender systems in which individual, acquired, and ascribed traits are more important in determining gender identity than is biological sex assignment." This could be applied to European prehistoric contexts as well.

3.7 Cultures, Migrations, and Diasporic Identities

As discussed in Section 1.1, an instrumentalist approach to ethnicity and cultural identity has prevailed in identity studies of the past few decades. Bioarchaeological data have much to contribute to these studies, as one line of evidence among several. While people's origins may be revealed through genes and isotopes, and ethnicity claims are rooted in those origins, ethnicity and origins are not isomorphic. Just as archaeologists have become increasingly nuanced in how they interpret the observable patterning of material culture for reconstructions of group identity, bioarchaeologists can do the same. It used to be the case that the material culture was the solid evidence, and a group's origins were a matter of inference and speculation. Now the perception is that the reverse is true, so that the genetic data is seen as even more solid evidence, while the material culture could be manipulated or negotiated (which post-processualists have long argued). While scholars are rightly concerned that this perception that genes can on their own reveal ethnic affiliation is dangerous, it is also the case that genetic evidence often does not answer the questions we archaeologists are asking. The data written on the body is not the final answer to questions of identity; it is merely a portion of the story, and one must then triangulate the archaeological and genetic records to understand how cultural groups formed. In Semerari et al.'s (2021) study of the first millennium BCE Mediterranean, the authors note that "material cultural data may point to the existence of discrete territories and cultural boundaries where bioarchaeological analyses see a more continuous genetic signature, heavily influenced by gene flow between individuals and groups." This does not make the culturally derived collective identities any less meaningful, but it does demonstrate that the material and bioarchaeological records are best studied together to obtain a more complete picture of past cultural identities.

Genetic data from Dolní Věstonice II may have been useful for revealing kinship but offers nothing on cultural identity. The mitochondrial DNA of all the human remains from Dolní Věstonice II whose mtDNA could be extracted successfully (n.=6, including the triple burial) belong to the U haplogroup, very characteristic of European hunter-gatherer populations before the Neolithic. This supports a picture of a relatively genetically homogenous population across the continent prior to the arrival of farming peoples (Mittnik and Krause 2016: 383). But this information is so far removed from the emic experience of these individuals that one is inclined to say it says nothing about identity at all – certainly nothing about any purported cultural groups.

This disconnect between genetic evidence and identity is evident in work at Pompeii, Italy. There, the Casa del Fabbro is a dwelling that has yielded a rich body of material as well as a complex architectural history. There was a contraction in the size and sumptuousness of the house in the years immediately prior to the eruption of Vesuvius in 79 CE. At the time of the eruption, storage units of personal belongings were stashed in the public rooms of the house, there was only one couch in the main dining room instead of the expected three, a latrine had been placed just inside the entrance, and the wall paintings in the once-gracious house had not been maintained. The overall impression is "that the house had come on harder times, or at least that it had passed into the hands of an owner or tenant with different cultural standards." (Ling et al. 1997: 150). A substantial set of tools that could have belonged to a carpenter, a surgeon, or even a scrap merchant hints at the owner's occupation. While the picture remains murky, the artifacts and the space itself suggest the last owner was a specialized craftsperson, likely a male given the tools, who had either lost status or was a new owner of a formerly elite dwelling. This is gleaned by traditional archaeological means. A study of the genome of one of the two bodies found in the house, in fact the first individual genome sequenced from Pompeii, added little new. The DNA of Individual A, a biologically sexed male, "shows a higher level of shared genetic drift with the central Italy Roman Imperial Age group" than with other groups, so the authors infer that he came from the Italian peninsula (Scorrano et al. 2022). We learn that 80 percent of his ancestry was derived from Anatolian and Iranian Neolithic farmers, with a small amount of steppe-related genes (reflecting post-Neolithic dispersals) and an even smaller amount of European hunter-gatherer (WHG) components. But this distant ancestry would have been unknown and irrelevant to Individual A. The same study did include osteological analysis, which revealed that Individual A suffered from spinal tuberculosis (Pott's Disease) a diagnosis which was indirectly confirmed by the genetic study (Scorrano et al. 2022). This last piece of information is certainly important for understanding more about the person's lived experience, but the aDNA adds nothing to the cultural identity that we already could infer from the material culture: This person was Roman.

The futility of using aDNA to reveal cultural identity is also evident in the context of the Aegean Bronze Age. Archaeologically defined cultural groups, the Mycenaeans on the Greek mainland and the Minoans on Crete, have proven to be impossible to differentiate genetically because of the common genetic pool across the Aegean (Richards et al. 2022). But for Maran (2022) and others, because the labels of Mycenaean and Minoan are artificial inventions by modern scholars, the entire enterprise of measuring the genetic evidence against these groups is flawed: There was never a Mycenaean or Minoan identity to prove or disprove! Thus, by not absorbing the lessons of archaeological identity studies, archaeogeneticists can end up reproducing simplistic and literal conceptions of past cultural groups.

Whether demographic groupings are culturally derived, biological, or neither, we are interested in when, where, and how people move, and what happens when they do. The isotopic data are useful here. Of course, mobility need not be the norm. Leppard et al. (2020) studied circumscribed movements in the Mediterranean on a macroscale: They used strontium isotope data to show that only 5–10 percent of all skeletons whose isotopes were analyzed died in a location different from their place of birth; in other words, 90 percent or more of individuals in ancient cemeteries were local. Moreover, the percentage of nonlocals progressively decreased after the Neolithic. Although Perry et al. (2022) found significant errors in Leppard et al.'s study, their results independently confirmed the original study's overall patterns. Leppard et al. infer that most people did not move much in antiquity, and the purported Mediterranean connectivity was reserved for a select few.

In the Alpine region, Ötzi moved around but apparently stayed local. The strontium and oxygen isotopic signatures of Ötzi's dental enamel fit with his surrounding location, suggesting he was born in the general region where he died, more precisely in one of the valleys within 60 km of his findspot (Müller et al. 2003). However, his bones indicated he had spent the past 10–20 years living somewhere else, either at a higher altitude or northwest of his birth-place, or perhaps moving frequently out of the region (Müller et al. 2003). Ötzi the Iceman's movements are of intellectual interest, without eliciting wide-spread controversy.

Long-distance permanent migrations are another matter, as the debates over how the technology of agriculture spread into Europe at the Mesolithic-Neolithic transition from the seventh to fourth millennium BCE demonstrate. While the first salvos of Ammerman and Cavalli Sforza (1971, 1973) were met with skepticism by archaeologists, the story told by the genetic evidence has won out. This debate has been pretty conclusively resolved in favor of the demic diffusion of Near Eastern farmers west into Europe, rather than the diffusion of farming technologies alone (Chikhi et al. 2002). Acceptance followed a slow series of concessions from claims of a combination of migration and accultur-ation (Thomas 2006: 53) to a recognition that the population replacement that came with the introduction of agriculture in Europe was near total. Nonetheless, the Neolithicization of Europe was far from a juggernaut, as there were areas where peoples who engaged in different subsistence practices coexisted and intermingled for long periods (Borić 2005). Furthermore, even total genetic absorption need not mean erasure of preexisting cultural knowledge – far from it. Consider Ötzi, an embodiment of both Neolithic lifeways and of region-specific knowledge of wild plants and animals. He demonstrates the preserva-tion of local hunter-gatherer practices after the transition to agriculture. But Ötzi's DNA in both his maternal and paternal lineage reveals origins among Near Eastern farmers who migrated in the early part of the Neolithic, starting c. 7000 BCE: In fact, a newly generated high-coverage genome shows that fully 90 percent of Ötzi's ancestry derives from Anatolian farmers, with very little European hunter-gatherer (WHG) (Sikora et al. 2014; Wang et al. 2023). Does this information about Ötzi's DNA tell us who he is, to borrow Reich's title? Hardly. Ötzi's DNA is not reflected in his lifestyle or his skillset, utterly adapted to Alpine living. This highlights a key and somewhat paradoxical limitation of aDNA: While it reveals long-term human history, it only has a real-world relevance for as long as people retain a memory of their origins. The timescale of identity afforded by archaeogenetic data is vanishingly short – a matter of a few generations. After that, for the thousands of years that follow, the genetic sequences are irrelevant except perhaps now, when, for ourselves, we can find out this information.

One consequence of knowing through genetic data that there was a movement of people in a particular place and time is how this changes our understanding of the visibility of the migrants' material culture. Identifying migrants from their material possessions is not a numbers game, whereby the bigger the group of migrants the greater their visibility. Migrations that take the form of settler-colonialism as in Europeans to the Americas, Greeks and Phoenicians to the central and western Mediterranean, or Arabs to Africa in the medieval period, leave extensive traces of materials either imported from the homeland or made locally in the style of their place of origin. Even if their numbers are small, if the new arrivals wield political or economic power, sometimes or perhaps usually the local populations will absorb elements of the new material culture and practices, over time.

Archaeological studies of diasporic identities have applied this model and relied on fairly straightforward material culture analyses (see Knapp 2021: 8 for a list of material correlates of migrants). A well-documented case is an enclave of two houses of Etruscan merchants at the ancient port city of Lattara in southern France, which flourished in the mid-first millennium BCE. The identification of two houses' occupants as Etruscan is based on the large quantities of Etruscan ceramics, both household cookwares and the transport amphora that apparently signal the owners' livelihood, as well as Etruscan graffiti on numerous vessels. The quantities are significant in their own right but especially compared to the absence of these materials in other households in this town of native and Greek colonial inhabitants (Dietler 2010). This is as close to a textbook example of the archaeological demonstration of displaced members of an ethnic group in antiquity as we can hope for. With a big enough dispersal of such clusters over a wide area, the term diaspora may be applied (Lilley 2004).

The first macroscale genetic study of early Medieval burials in England highlights a more complex case of heterogeneous populations only partly revealed by the material culture. Gretzinger et al. (2022) analyzed the DNA from 278 individuals from 21 cemeteries across England from the fifth to ninth centuries CE. While the authors succeeded in detecting the Anglo-Saxon migrations into southeast England through the genetic material, laying to rest a longstanding debate, this did not resolve questions of identity but instead raised new ones. The grave goods did not display ethnicity or even cultural identity in any consistent or clear-cut way. This demonstrates what we have known, that people's origins, especially a couple generations on, may influence but do not determine lived identity. First of all, the groups were interacting: "Although most individuals from early medieval English sites cluster clearly with either present-day WBI [western British or Irish] samples or CNEs [continental northern Europeans], many individuals fall between these two clusters, suggesting admixture between these ancestral groups." (Gretzinger et al. 2022: 113). Aligning the grave goods and burial types with these mixed populations, even within the same family, is far from straightforward. Nor did geographic origin determine status in any obvious way. The authors found "individuals of both ancestries within prominent and/or furnished burials" (Gretzinger et al. 2022: 114). While females of continental origin were buried more often with brooches than their British counterparts, males of both origins could be buried with weapons. If within a few generations there is already admixture, and if cultural origin did not track with status, we can see the relatively rapid unraveling of cultural difference, at least as expressed archaeologically.

Indeed, this process can happen even more quickly. Recent archaeological and anthropological work on the relationship between contemporary migrants, their possessions, and their sense of place has revealed that migrants will shed every possession they hold dear, every material vestige of their origins, if that is necessary for survival and the success of their journey. Gokee and De León (2014: 146, Table 3) in their study of recently formed migrant assemblages in the Sonoran Desert along the US-Mexico border found virtually no possessions in the traditional sense, with personal items making up less than 2% of the artifacts. In a survey of migrant assemblages in western Sicily, Robert Schon and this author documented similar results, with personal objects making up just 2.4% of the assemblages (2019: 189, Table 6). This pattern led Blake and Schon (2019) to suggest that archaeologists would do well to rethink the relationship between possessions and identity. In a series of interviews conducted with migrants in Athens, Stephanie Martin documented how migrants barely spoke of *things* at all when recounting their journeys from their homeland. The only exception in contemporary cases is the cell phone – for practical purposes but also for communication with family in the home country (Martin 2023: 11). One lesson from this is methodological, that we cannot expect to find group identities through material possessions in all circumstances and therefore may miss, for example, diasporic enclaves. But the pattern may demonstrate something more profound: that not only can personal possessions be shed in extreme circumstances, but perhaps aspects of identities can be shed as well. In other words, the detachment from material possessions (whether forced or voluntary) may weaken one's sense of belonging to certain groups. Whether one accepts that last point or not, the reality is that the endeavor of getting at the cultural identity of displaced (as opposed to simply mobile or nomadic) groups from their material traces is complex. Within a few generations, genetic origin may be entirely forgotten and immaterial.

3.7.1 Case Study: The Bell Beaker Phenomenon

The Bell Beaker phenomenon, a classic example of the archaeological struggle to link artifacts and identity, is a case in point. The changing terminology tells the story: There is the Beaker Folk (securely an ethnic group (Harrison 1980)); bell beaker culture (Harrison 1974) (a coherent archaeological culture); bell beaker complex (Besse and Strahm 2001) (no longer a unitary group but still implying a correlation between population groupings, ideology, and material culture); bell beaker package or set (Manasterski et al. 2020) (a focus on goods and ideas but not people) and, currently, bell beaker phenomenon (Derenne et al. 2022), which sidesteps any claims of material representations of collective identity.

As described in the Introduction, the clay bell-shaped vessels found as grave goods in Western Europe in the third millennium BCE have confounded scholars for a century or more (Figures 4 and 5). Their distribution is too uneven and patchy in the territory where they are found to make a case for a single geographically bounded cultural group, so how to explain them? The deceased in the graves containing the beakers are inhumations, in some regions more often male, but in Iberia the beakers are fairly evenly represented in female graves as well. They are sometimes accompanied by copper objects including tanged daggers, palmela points, awls, ivory v-perforated buttons, and more (Soriano et al. 2021). The graves in all cases seem to coexist with or replace older burial practices, rather than evolving organically from local traditions.

For many decades in the twentieth century, a culture-historical narrative of diffusion of these ceramics from a single point of origin predominated, with Castillo's (1928) theory of an Iberian origin being perennially popular and notably reaffirmed in Case (2004). According to this narrative, the beakers were the identity markers of peoples who migrated and introduced their culture to the populations they encountered. The advent of radiocarbon dating complicated this picture, as the absolute dates did not support a single early origin in Iberia with subsequent spread from there. Responding to the dating evidence, Harrison (1974) and others posited a double origin for the beakers, one in the Rhineland and another in Iberia known as the Maritime Beaker group, but advocated for independent local types originating autochthonously within those two broad complexes. In this processual perspective, no people were moving with the beakers.

Besides the debate over whether or not beakers were stand-ins for an ethnic group, there was an apparent technological component as well, as the spread of the beakers maps, in northwest Europe at least, onto the spread of copper technology. In Central Europe copper was in use for a millennium by the time beakers appeared, and there is no distinction between beaker copper and non-beaker copper there, based on trace element analysis (Merkl 2010). In northwest Europe, in contrast, the technology and the artifact types apparently arrive together. This contemporaneity has been pushed further to suggest that a component of "bell beaker ideology" (as Merkl 2010: 20 put it) was a valuation of copper.

The impact of postprocessual archaeology was evident in new theories concerning the beakers which emerged in the 1980s and 1990s. The beaker distribution came to be framed as a "package" of goods and ideas that spread around Europe and was centered on a particular construction of masculinity that reached the level of a cult (e.g. Sherratt 1987). In this reading, the identity being expressed by the artifacts of the beaker package – primarily a drinking, warring maleness – was gender, not ethnicity. While some scholars were still willing to entertain the notion of at least some people moving, the mechanisms for the diffusions of this package were downplayed. As Brodie (1997: 305–306) notes, "Copper working was most likely carried to Britain by small groups of Beaker migrants but its earlier or contemporary importation into north-west Europe and the Rhine Valley was by other means – by a process which would normally be described as 'cultural diffusion' or 'a flow of ideas'."

Brodie (1997) also rejected the prevailing theory that the Beaker package reflected a male-only cult. The ceramic beakers themselves are found in graves of biologically sexed females as well as males, and with adults and children alike. However, weapons such as the tanged daggers predominate in adult male graves and copper awls show association in adult female graves, with children lacking such tools and weapons. Nonetheless, there is always a significant number of exceptions to this pattern. For example, the awls are considered a "female" implement because of their associations with female beaker burials, but in Iberia, with a distribution of 70 percent of awls in female graves and 30 percent in male graves, they are hardly exclusively female. Furthermore, only 29 percent of female graves contain awls (Soriano et al. 2021: 9). Status differences are also at work, apparently, with grave goods in addition to beakers correlating with grave size to suggest some wealth differentiation in these communities (Soriano et al. 2021: 2). Thus, beakers and their associated objects may represent numerous identity valences. Brodie (1997: 300) nonetheless sums up, perplexedly, "It seems true that many of the objects placed in a Beaker grave seem to have been indexical in that they marked out a social persona, whether real or ideal, but the Beaker pot itself was not part of this signification. It cross-cut all dimensions of social differentiation which it is possible to examine." Brodie goes on to argue, drawing on ethnographic parallels, for the inherent femaleness of beakers as products of female labor and the female symbolism of pottery vessels. We are by now a long way from discussions of how beakers spread around Europe in the first place.

All these theories remained speculative until Olalde et al.'s stunning 2018 genomic study. The aDNA of skeletons from beaker burials across Europe demonstrated convincingly that the beaker phenomenon originated in the eastern steppe regions and spread in complex ways westward and south. In Iberia the spread of the beaker complex was due to cultural transmission without migration. In Britain, it was due to migrations of men and women from continental Europe from around 2450 BCE, which resulted in near total population replacement by 2000 BCE. In Central and Western Europe, beakers arrived via a combination of some population movements from the steppe regions and some cultural transmission. An example of this complexity comes from Szigetszentmiklós, Hungary, where the researchers "found roughly contemporary Beaker-complex-associated individuals with very different proportions (from 0 percent to 75 percent) of steppe-related ancestry" (Olalde et al. 2018: 191–92). According to the authors, the genetic differences in the same community point to what was likely the early phase when new arrivals lived among local farmers.

This study settled many of the debates around the beakers and identity but was not without blowback. Furholt (2018) critiques the archaeogeneticists' emphasis on "single-event-mass-migrations" in interpretations of aDNA evidence of a tiny sample of ancient skeletons. Frieman and Hoffman (2019: 534) note that in the discussions of large scale migrations of the past, the catalysts for movement are poorly theorized, converging on "a one-dimensional view of migrations as a form of crisis response: something atypical and disruptive that will only be attempted when the evidently preferable alternative of staying put will no longer work." The crisis-response model certainly does not fit with the beaker case, where careful maintenance of material culture traditions and comparative wealth of the beaker graves suggest a movement made not in desperation but for opportunity. Armit and Reich (2021) dig into the British beaker evidence from the Olalde et al. study to propose an alternative explanation to the mass migration theory of beakers there, suggesting a more gradual westward demographic shift across Europe that they call "Steppe drift."

New questions arise following Olalde et al.'s study: Knowing conclusively that in some areas locals adopted the beaker package while in others there was a population change, can we distinguish differences in the beaker assemblages that reflect that? Can we detect cross-generational differences in presentation, and especially, what happens a few generations down the line from the migration? Thus, the genetic evidence opens up new archaeological questions concerning cultural identity and remembered origins following migration.

Zooming out from the Beaker assemblages, the evidence derived from new biomolecular techniques applied to human and animal remains is transforming the study of past identities in radical ways. Whether confirming or adding detail to extant studies of particular identity valences, or overturning prior understandings of others, this work is insuring the central place of identity studies in anthropological archaeology.

4 Identity Studies in the Twenty-First Century: Loose Ends and Future Directions

Despite the influx of new data to inform archaeological identity studies, there remain two critical issues that neither ontological approaches nor new bioarchaeological methods have resolved: The problem of the individual, and identity theory's conflicting handling of agency and structure. I argue that the resolution of those overlapping issues will move identity studies forward, with broader implications for anthropological archaeology.

4.1 What To Do About Individuals

> The narrative of a life can be understood as a building block of social history, allowing our scales of analysis to shift between big questions of populations and social change, on the one hand, and the events and contingencies at work across a single life, on the other.
>
> —Hosek and Robb 2019: 10

Archaeological identity studies' weak engagement with intersectionality is entwined with the field's ambivalence towards studying individuals in the archaeological record. From processualism on, anthropological archaeologists have considered individual people only for how they inform about their society, the goal being, to paraphrase Kent Flannery (1967: 120), "to find the system behind both the person and the artifact." Scholars from time to time bemoan this lack of interest in individual actors – a perspective encapsulated in Tringham's "faceless blobs" (1991: 94) – but as a social science the questions of our discipline always necessarily go beyond one person's experience, especially since we rarely have enough detail to explore a person in a fine-grained way. This resistance to writing about individuals in their own right puts the field at odds with the general public for whom ancient individuals – preferably named or nicknamed – are deeply compelling. But beyond that, a dismissal of individuals makes intersectional approaches challenging to implement: The convergence of multiple categories of identity is best witnessed in individuals.

Furthermore, while we are able to study groups and make inferences back to individuals who would belong to those groups (even if they are the faceless blobs), we have great difficulty making inferences going the other direction, from the individual to the group. Of course, this was a problem before the advent of modern identity studies. As Diaz-Andreu and Lucy (2005: 4) put it of the processual approaches to the individual, "The individual was very much part and parcel of the group, passive and obedient to its norms and pressures." We have not gotten beyond that. While the dialectic between agency and structure is fundamentally about the individual and society, we can handle generic "agents" far better than specific individuals. As a result, identity studies scholars, like agency theorists, have shown little interest in particular individuals. Although Insoll (2007: 3) notes that "the very idea of individual identity is something of a recent construct," there should be a way to apply identity theories at the level of the individual, as the nexus of multiple identity valences.

Bioarchaeological approaches offer a clear path forward to explore intersectional individuals (DeWitte and Yaussy 2020). One branch of scholarship, osteobiography, juxtaposes the individual and their life history with population-level data, thus offering a window into larger cultures and into nonnormative behaviors. It could thus provide a framework for intersectionality in prehistoric periods (Hosek and Robb 2019), and for the identification of nonbinary individuals (Hollimon 2017). This new data has not led to a rush to discuss individuals however. While this reluctance dovetails with current posthumanist approaches concerned with relational personhood over individuals, it has deeper roots in an even larger debate in anthropological archaeology, between agency and structure.

4.2 Is Identity Agency or Structure?

Hidden behind the demonstrated stability of identity studies in archaeology is a cleavage between understandings of how identity functions in society. This cleavage is directly tied to the perennial debate in anthropological archaeology over the relative importance of agency and structure in shaping society. This debate centers on the question to what extent are humans agents capable of transformative actions, and to what extent are people constrained by the circumstances of their lives, by the structures around them such as environment and institutions? Those who place the balance on the former, on agency, see humans as intentional actors with some autonomy. Those who think structure is determinative see humans replicating the structures around them. Discussions of agency closely track with those of identity, including the question of intentions, and of the individual versus the group. Thus, when Dobres and Robb (2000: 11) describe a commonly held position "that agency is less about the intentional exercise of personal interests and more about a cultural process through which personhood and a sense of 'groupness' are constructed, negotiated, and transformed," the word identity could be substituted for agency easily.

Identity studies in their first two decades focused on intentions and motivations, often suggesting that identity is a strong motivator for individual agents:

People do things in order to express who they are. Bioarchaeology on the other hand reveals some of the actions that identify categories of people in the past – such as what they ate, where they traveled, their stockrearing practices – without the intentions. For archaeologists and bioarchaeologists alike, repeated, routinized actions in the past are the most visible ones, and yet these are the actions that most suggest the power of structures. To give a hypothetical example, once one establishes that a particular biologically sexed female was a transhumant herder of local sheep who ate mostly terrestrial animals, it becomes difficult – or even seemingly beside the point – to add that she could have performed her femininity or that her cultural identity was meaningful. But actions without intentions are just behaviors: Responses to external stimuli. Behaviors are thus instantiations of structure, while intentions emphasize the agents within the structure. This divide for the most part goes unacknowledged because the term identity conflates the distinction between agency-centered scholarship and structure-framed scholarship. It is evident in the research itself, however. The verbs used in standard archaeological identity theory emphasize intentions of an autonomous self: constituting, expressing, maintaining, constructing, negotiating, and displaying. These verbs are at cross-purposes with the language of behavior that grounds the people encountered in, say, isotope studies: eating, drinking, childrearing, and traveling.

The way around this cleavage between agency and structure is not to claim either/or but both. After all, ancient peoples must have engaged in both types of actions, sometimes simultaneously. Do we need any more articles focused on Neolithic personhood, without acknowledging lifeways? Do we need isotope-derived inferences of patrilocalism that do not also address the inevitable familial fault lines in such a community? Interestingly, many years ago Ian Hodder (2000: 26) offered a blueprint of sorts for fusing the two types of actions in a focus on the individual: He proposed a study of the individual as a means of animating structural conditions, because "the structures are worked out and reproduced in the bodies of historical lives." (2000: 26).

Despite Hosek and Robb's (2019: 4–5) caution regarding "celebrity bodies," we can return to Ötzi, certainly the prehistoric European we know best. Hodder saw in Ötzi's movements between upland and lowland, and between times on his own, self-sufficient, and times in communities he would have encountered in the valleys, instantiations of "large scale transformations in economy, society and ideology [that] could only be achieved through the actions of individuals as they worked through the dichotomies of older systems and the practical world in which they lived their daily lives" (2000: 27). Hodder's take on the Iceman as an individual does not in fact concern his identity. We could attach all sorts of identity categories to Ötzi: male, older adult, hunter, alpine dweller, sometime vegetarian, expert naturalist, murder victim, Copper Age person, European, and heart-disease sufferer. Yet in the reconstructions of Ötzi's actions, meals, and possessions in the days and hours leading up to his death, no one explains his decisions to drink water from this or that mountain stream (Rott 2000), or to carry birch fungus (Peintner and Pöder 2000) or to hike above the treeline, as identity-driven. What happened to him – his murder – could have been identity driven; indeed must have been in the most basic sense that he was the one killed and not another person. But in terms of his own behavior, it would seem that if intentional identity worked at all here, it was not the most important factor driving his actions, which were instead shaped by externalities and his bank of practical knowledge. Certainly his decision-making was colored by his identity as an alpine dweller who knew that he could safely survive in a remote high-altitude location, but this takes us a long way from saying his actions were identity-driven. Even his tattoos, those most expressive of body modifications, were not apparently messages of identity but therapeutic (Samadelli et al. 2015; see Krutak 2019 for an indigenous ontological take on tattooing). Rather than someone performing their identity and generating themselves through their actions, appearance, and possessions, truly a fundamental tenet of identity studies, we see in Ötzi the pressures and constraints of externalities that determined his behavior.

Leaning into the notion that humans are both agents of change and products of structural conditions is necessary for a mature identity theory to emerge, one that can engage with prehistoric intersectional individuals. In fact, there is more at stake than intersectionality. By recognizing that people in the past and present act(ed) in ways that often have nothing to do with any self-aware identity is not to deprive them of autonomy. Instead, accepting humans as also the products of structural conditions can allow for the absorption of a key insight of posthumanism, that of relational personhood. In doing this, we need not forego the richness of narratives of individual lives; rather, we can weave them into an equally rich tapestry of natural, social, and material worlds.

4.3 Concluding Thoughts

For more than thirty years, identity writ large has served as a foundation for much archaeological fieldwork and interpretation. If not a paradigm in the Kuhnian sense, identity studies certainly are a school of archaeological theory. After a time, a crumbling of disciplinary consensus was to be expected, as the field had pretty much exhausted the ways we could use material culture to infer identities in the past. A new generation of archaeologists sought fresh theories, ones that did not concern human identity at all, shifting the discussion to artifacts in their own right and ontological approaches that reject the distinction between human and nonhuman altogether. In a competitive field in which new theories aid professional advancement, the demise of identity theory would seem inevitable. Yet something unexpected overturned this normal trajectory: Just at the point when identity theory was poised to decline, an explosion of new data derived from methodological breakthroughs in biomolecular approaches flooded the field with information on exactly the topic of human identity The result is that the study of identity remains a stable and central component of anthropological archaeology, alongside traditional scholarly topics such as social organization or political economy. Identity's perennial, indeed super-charged importance in the eyes of the public combined with the injection of masses of new data has ensured identity's survival after its abandonment by archaeological theorists. Furthermore, some aspects of posthumanism have improved identity studies. Acknowledging that Western notions of bounded individuals are not universal opens up new interpretations that can only improve identity studies. In particular, the recognition that past peoples may have been partible or granted personhood to animals would seem to explain otherwise perplexing material assemblages. In light of the continued public interest in identity, the new techniques for detecting it, and the theoretical innovations that posthumanist approaches may provide, identity studies will flourish for the foreseeable future. This is a good thing, because identity studies allow for explanations of certain aspects of the archaeological record without recourse to functionalism or ideology. While a mature field of identity studies will not purport to explain everything, it can explain some things very well.

So what have identity studies taught us? In spite of some unsettled issues concerning archaeological individuals, behavior and action, agency and struc-ture, there is much to celebrate in the achievements of identity studies. We now recognize the indigenous role in colonialist interactions, which resolves the question of why, if empires imposed ideology and culture with force, there was always significant and patterned variation in the material record within those empires. We've severed biological sex and socially constructed gender fairly conclusively, so that any observed congruency between the two must be proven not assumed. We've determined that a drive for belonging and group identity can cause old traditions to endure or be revived or even invented. We've come to recognize that status is not simply expressed but is performed and negotiated, and that far from merely reflecting one's social position, material culture is harnessed to do this work of status performance. We've learned that valences of identity will intersect, and so the experiences of an elite Gallo-Roman woman will be fundamentally different from a female enslaved person in Roman Sicily. And we have learned that the groups we called the Vikings or the Romans are not unitary, but composed of individuals with different experiences, lifestyles, and even origins. Moreover, such groups are not the point of departure for action, they are a dynamic outcome of internal and external actions and pressures. Perhaps most importantly, we have recognized that our own positionality and professional and personal identities color our studies of the past and determine the reception of those studies. All these statements, now so commonplace, have moved the field of anthropological archaeology forward. The rich data emerging from bioarchaeological methods does more than just add detail to the statements above. To the enthusiasm of some and consternation of others, it is destabilizing the primacy of material culture as the source of our interpretations of the people of the past. Yet engagement with all sorts of data is essential for identity studies to mature within anthropological archaeology, thus contributing to making our interpretations of the elusive past, always imperfect and incomplete, ring a little more true.

References

Adamesteanu, D. (1958). Butera: Piano della Fiera, consi e fontana calda. *Monumenti Antichi*, *44*, 205–672.

Agarwal, S. C. (2012). The past of sex, gender, and health: Bioarchaeology of the aging skeleton. *American Anthropologist*, *114*(2), 322–35, https://doi.org/10.1111/j.1548-1433.2012.01428.x.

Agarwal, S. C. & Wesp, J. K., eds. (2017). *Exploring Sex and Gender in Bioarchaeology*. Albuquerque: University of New Mexico Press.

Agnew, A. M. & Justus, H. M. (2014). Preliminary investigations of the bioarchaeology of medieval Giecz (XI-XII c.): Examples of trauma and stress. *Anthropological Review*, *77*(2), 189–203, https://doi.org/10.2478/anre-2014-0015.

Alberti, B. (2016). Archaeologies of ontology. *Annual Review of Anthropology*, *45*, 163–79, https://doi.org/10.1146/annurev-anthro-102215-095858.

Alt, K. W., Pichler, S., Vach, W. et al. (1997). Twenty-five thousand-year-old triple burial from Dolní Věstonice: An ice-age family? *American Journal of Physical Anthropology: The Official Publication of the American Association of Physical Anthropologists*, *102*(1), 123–31, https://doi.org/10.1002/(SICI)1096-8644(199701)102:1<123::AID-AJPA10>3.0.CO;2-2.

Ammerman, A. J. & Cavalli-Sforza, L. L. (1971). Measuring the rate of spread of early farming in Europe. *Man*, *6*, 674–88.

Ammerman, A. J. & Cavalli-Sforza, L. L. (1973). A population model for the diffusion of farming into Europe. In A. C. Renfrew, ed., *The Explanation of Culture Change: Models in Prehistory*. London: Duckworth, pp. 343–58.

Amundsen-Meyer, L., Engel, N. & Pickering, S., eds. (2011). Identity crisis: Archaeological perspectives on social identity. *42nd Annual Chacmool Archaeology Conference*, University of Calgary, Alberta, https://dx.doi.org/10.11575/PRISM/37038.

Armit, I. & Reich, D. (2021). The return of the Beaker folk? Rethinking migration and population change in British prehistory. *Antiquity*, *95*(384), 1464–77.

Arnold, B. (1990). The past as propaganda: Totalitarian archaeology in Nazi Germany. *Antiquity*, *64*(244), 464–78.

Arnold, B. (1999). "Drinking the feast": Alcohol and the legitimation of power in Celtic Europe. *Cambridge Archaeological Journal*, *9*(1), 71–93.

Ashmore, W. & Knapp, A. B., eds. (1999). *Archaeologies of Landscape: Contemporary Perspectives*. London: Blackwell.

Atalay, S. (2012). *Community-Based Archaeology: Research with, by, and for Indigenous and Local Communities*. Berkeley: University of California Press.

Bacon, B., Khatiri, A., Palmer, J. et al. (2023). An upper Paleolithic proto-writing system and phenological calendar. *Cambridge Archaeological Journal, 33*(3), 371–89, https://doi.org/10.1017/S0959774322000415.

Barrett, J. C., Bradley, R. J. & Green, M. (1991). *Landscape, Monuments and Society: The Prehistory of Cranborne Chase*. Cambridge: Cambridge University Press.

Barth, F., ed. (1969). *Ethnic Groups and Boundaries: The Social Organization of Culture Difference*. Boston: Little Brown and Co.

Baxter, J. E. (2022). *The Archaeology of Childhood*. Lanham, MD: Rowman & Littlefield.

Bentley, R. A. (2006). Strontium isotopes from the earth to the archaeological skeleton: A review. *Journal of Archaeological Method and Theory, 13*, 135–87, https://doi.org/10.1007/s10816-006-9009-x.

Berecki, S. (2014). The coexistence and interference of the late Iron Age Transylvanian communities. In C. N. Popa and S. Stoddart, eds., *Fingerprinting the Iron Age: Approaches to Identity in the European Iron Age: Integrating South-Eastern Europe into the Debate*. Oxford: Oxbow Books, pp. 11–17.

Besse, M. & Strahm, C. (2001). The components of the Bell Beaker complex. In F. Nicolis, ed., *Bell Beakers Today: Pottery, People, Culture, Symbols in Prehistoric Europe*, 1, *Proceedings of the International Colloquium Riva Del Garda*. Trento: Edizioni All'Insegna del Giglio, pp. 103–10.

Blackmore, C. (2011). How to queer the past without sex: Queer theory, feminisms and the archaeology of identity. *Archaeologies: Journal of the World Archaeological Congress, 7*(1), 75–96.

Blake, E. (1998). Sardinia's Nuraghi: Four millennia of becoming. *World Archaeology, 30*(1), 59–71, www.jstor.org/stable/125009.

Blake, E. (2014). *Social Networks and Regional Identity in Bronze Age Italy*. Cambridge: Cambridge University Press.

Blake, E., & Schon, R. (2019). The Archaeology of Contemporary Migrant Journeys in Western Sicily. *Journal of Mediterranean Archaeology, 32*(2).

Borić, D. (2005). Fuzzy horizons of change: Orientalism and the frontier model of the Mesolithic-Neolithic transition. In N. Milner and P. Woodman, eds., *Mesolithic Studies at the Beginning of the 21st Century*. Oxford: Oxbow Books, pp. 81–105.

Bowes, K., ed. (2021). *The Roman Peasant Project 2009–2014: Excavating the Roman Rural Poor*, Vol. 154. Philadelphia: University of Pennsylvania, https://doi.org/10.2307/j.ctv18dvvqq.

Brandon, J. C. (2004). Reconstructing domesticity and segregating households: The intersections of gender and race in the postbellum south. In K. S. Barile and J. C. Brandon, eds., *Household Chores and Household Choices: Theorizing the Domestic Sphere in Historical Archaeology*, Tuscaloosa: University of Alabama Press, pp. 197–210.

Brodie, N. (1997). New perspectives on the Bell-Beaker culture. *Oxford Journal of Archaeology*, *16*(3), 297–314, https://doi.org/10.1111/1468-0092.00042.

Brubaker, R. & Cooper, F. (2000). Beyond "identity." *Theory and Society*, *29*, 1–47, www.jstor.org/stable/3108478.

Brück, J. (2005). Homing instincts: Grounded identities and dividual selves in the British Bronze Age. In E. C. Casella and C. Fowler, eds., *The Archaeology of Plural and Changing Identities*. Boston, MA: Springer, pp. 135–160.

Brück, J. (2021). Ancient DNA, kinship and relational identities in Bronze Age Britain. *Antiquity*, *95*(379), 228–37, https://doi.org/10.15184/aqy.2020.216.

Budd, P., Millard, A., Chenery, C., Lucy, S., Roberts, C. (2004). Investigating population movement by stable isotope analysis : a report from Britain. *Antiquity*, 78(299), 127–41.

Campbell, L., Maldonado, A., Pierce, E. & Russell, A., eds. (2016). *Creating Material Worlds: The Uses of Identity in Archaeology*. Oxford: Oxbow Books.

Canuto, M. A. & Yaeger, J. (2000). *Archaeology of Communities: A New World Perspective*. Abingdon: Routledge.

Case, H. (2004). Beakers and the Beaker culture. In J. Czebreszuk, ed., *Similar but Different: Bell Beakers in Europe*. Poznan: Adam Mickiewicz University Press, pp. 11–34.

Casella, E. & Fowler, C., eds. (2005). Beyond Identification. In Casella, E. and Fowler, C. eds., *The Archaeology of Plural and Changing Identities: Beyond Identification*. Boston: Springer, pp. 1–8.

Cassidy, L. M., Maoldúin, R. Ó., Kador, T. et al. (2020). A dynastic elite in monumental Neolithic society. *Nature*, *582*(7812), 384–88, https://doi.org/10.1038/s41586-020-2378-6.

Castillo Yurrita, A. (1928). *La cultura del vaso campaniforme (su origen y extensión en Europa)*. Barcelona: Universidad di Barcelona.

Chapman, J. (2000). *Fragmentation in Archaeology: People, Places and Broken Objects in the Prehistory of South Eastern Europe*. Abingdon: Routledge.

Chikhi, L., Nichols, R. A., Barbujani, G. & Beaumont, M. A. (2002). Y genetic data support the Neolithic demic diffusion model. *Proceedings of the*

National Academy of Sciences, *99*(17), 11008–13, https://doi.org/10.1073/pnas.162158799.

Collar, A. (2013). *Religious Networks in the Roman Empire: The Spread of New Ideas*. Cambridge: Cambridge University Press.

Conkey, M. W. & Spector, J. D. (1984). Archaeology and the study of gender. *Advances in Archaeological Method and Theory*, *7*, 1–38.

Connerton, P. (1989). *How Societies Remember*. Cambridge: Cambridge University Press.

Conway, B. (2003). Active remembering, selective forgetting, and collective identity: The case of Bloody Sunday. *Identity: An International Journal of Theory and Research*, *3*(4), 305–23, https://doi.org/10.1207/S1532706XID 0304_01.

Crellin, R. J. & Harris, O. J. (2020). Beyond binaries. Interrogating ancient DNA. *Archaeological Dialogues*, *27*(1), 37–56.

Crellin, R. J. & Harris, O. J. (2021). What difference does posthumanism make? *Cambridge Archaeological Journal*, *31*(3), 469–75, https://doi.org./10.1017/S0959774321000159.

Crenshaw, K. (1989). Demarginalizing the intersection of race and sex: A Black feminist critique of antidiscrimination doctrine, feminist theory, and antiracist politics. *University of Chicago Legal Forum*, *1989*(1), 139–67, http://chicagounbound.uchicago.edu/uclf/vol1989/iss1/8.

Crowder, K. D., Montgomery, J., Filipek, K. L. & Evans, J. A. (2020). Romans, barbarians and foederati: New biomolecular data and a possible region of origin for "Headless Romans" and other burials from Britain. *Journal of Archaeological Science: Reports*, *30*, 102180, https://doi.org/10.1016/j.jasrep.2019.102180.

De la Cadena, M. & Starn, O., eds. (2007). *Indigenous Experience Today*. Abingdon: Routledge.

Deleuze, G. & Guattari, F. (1987). *A Thousand Plateaus, Capitalism and Schizophrenia*. Translated by B. Massumi. Minneapolis: University of Minnesota Press.

Derenne, E., Ard, V. & Besse, M. (2022). Potters' mobility contributed to the emergence of the Bell Beaker phenomenon in Third Millennium BCE Alpine Switzerland: A diachronic technology study of domestic and funerary traditions. *Open Archaeology*, *8*(1), 925–55, https://doi.org/10.1515/opar-2022-0264.

DeWitte, S. & Yaussy, S. (2020). Bioarchaeological applications of intersectionality. In C. M. Cheverko, J. R. Prince-Buitenhuys and M. Hubbe, eds., *Theoretical Approaches in Bioarchaeology*, Abingdon: Routledge, pp. 45–58.

Díaz-Andreu, M. & Lucy, S. (2005). Introduction. In M. Díaz-Andreu, S. Lucy, S. Babić and D. N. Edwards, eds., *The Archaeology of Identity*, Abingdon: Routledge, pp. 1–12.

Dickson, J. H., Oeggl, K., Holden, T. G. et al. (2000). The omnivorous Tyrolean Iceman: Colon contents (meat, cereals, pollen, moss and whipworm) and stable isotope analyses. *Philosophical Transactions of the Royal Society of London: Series B, Biological Sciences*, *355*, 1843–49, https://doi.org/10.1098/rstb.2000.0739.

Dietler, M. (1999). Rituals of commensality and the politics of state formation in the "princely" societies of early Iron Age Europe. *Publications de l'École Française de Rome*, *252*(1), 135–52, https://doi.org/10.4000/books.pcjb.303.

Dietler, M. (2006). Alcohol: Anthropological/archaeological perspectives. *Annual Review of Anthropology*, *35*, 229–49, https://doi.org/10.1146/annurev.anthro.35.081705.123120.

Dietler, M. (2010). *Archaeologies of Colonialism: Consumption, Entanglement, and Violence in Ancient Mediterranean France*. Berkeley: University of California Press.

Dobres, M. A. & Robb, J. E. (2000). Agency in archaeology: Paradigm or platitude? In M. A. Dobres and J. E. Robb, eds., *Agency in Archaeology*, 1st ed., Abingdon: Routledge, pp. 3–17.

Duval, P. M. (1989). Pourquoi «nos ancêtres les Gaulois». *Publications de l'École Française de Rome*, *116*(1), 199–217.

Elliott, A., ed. (2011). *The Routledge Handbook of Identity Studies*. Abingdon: Routledge.

Ensor, B. E., Irish, J. D. & Keegan, W. F. (2017). The bioarchaeology of kinship: Proposed revisions to assumptions guiding interpretation. *Current Anthropology*, *58*(6), 739–61, www.jstor.org/stable/26547056.

Eriksen, M. H. (2020). "Body-objects" and personhood in the Iron and Viking Ages: Processing, curating, and depositing skulls in domestic space. *World Archaeology*, *52*, 103–19. https://doi.org/10.1080/00438243.2019.1741439.

Ervynck, A., Van Neer, W., Hüster-Plogmann, H. & Schibler, J. (2003). Beyond affluence: The zooarchaeology of luxury. *World Archaeology*, *34*(3), 428–41, www.jstor.org/stable/3560195.

Ferguson, L. (1992). *Uncommon Ground: Archaeology and Early African America, 1650–1800*. Washington, DC: Smithsonian Books.

Flannery, K. V. (1967). Culture history v. cultural process: A debate in American archaeology. *Scientific American*, *217*(2), 119–22.

Flohr, M. (2017). Constructing occupational identities in the Roman world. In K. Verboven and C. Laes, eds., *Work, Labour, and Professions in the Roman World*. Leiden: Brill, pp. 147–72.

Fogelin, L. (2019). *An Unauthorized Companion to Archaeological Theory.* Unpublished Book, www.academia.edu/40368859/An_Unauthorized_ Companion_To_American_Archaeological_Theory_PDF.

Formicola, V. (2007). From the Sunghir children to the Romito dwarf: Aspects of the Upper Paleolithic funerary landscape. *Current Anthropology, 48*(3), 446–53, https://doi.org/10.1086/517592.

Formicola, V., Pontrandolfi, A. & Svoboda, J. (2001). The Upper Paleolithic triple burial of Dolní Věstonice: Pathology and funerary behavior. *American Journal of Physical Anthropology: The Official Publication of the American Association of Physical Anthropologists, 115*(4), 372–79, https://doi.org/ 10.1002/ajpa.1093.

Fowler, C. (2004). *The Archaeology of Personhood: An Anthropological Approach.* New York: Routledge.

Fowler, C. (2005). Identity politics: Personhood, kinship, gender and power in neolithic and early bronze age Britain. In E. C. Casella and C. Fowler, eds., *The Archaeology of Plural and Changing Identities.* Boston, MA: Springer, pp. 109–34.

Fowler, C. (2010). From identity and material culture to personhood and materiality. In D. Hicks and M. C. Beaudry, eds, *The Oxford Handbook of Material Culture Studies.* Oxford: Oxford University Press, pp. 352–85.

Fowles, S. (2016). The perfect subject (postcolonial object studies). *Journal of Material Culture, 21*(1), 9–27, https://doi.org/10.1177/1359183515623818.

Franklin, M. (2001). A black feminist-inspired archaeology? *Journal of Social Archaeology, 1*(1), 10–25, https://doi.org/10.1177/146960530100100108.

Frayer, D., Nava, A., Tartaglia, G. et al. (2020). Evidence for labret use in prehistory. *Bulletin of the International Association for Paleodontology, 14* (1), 1–23, https://hrcak.srce.hr/ojs/index.php/paleodontology/article/view/ 10565.

French, J. C., & Nowell, A. (2022). Growing up Gravettian: Bioarchaeological perspectives on adolescence in the European mid-Upper Paleolithic. *Journal of Anthropological Archaeology, 67,* 101430.

Frieman, C. J. & Hofmann, D. (2019). Present pasts in the archaeology of genetics, identity, and migration in Europe: A critical essay. *World Archaeology, 51*(4), 528–45, https://doi.org/10.1080/00438243.2019.1627907.

Fu, Q., Mittnik, A., Johnson, P. L. et al. (2013). A revised timescale for human evolution based on ancient mitochondrial genomes. *Current Biology, 23*(7), 553–59, https://doi.org/10.1016/j.cub.2013.02.044.

Furholt, M. (2018). Massive migrations? The impact of recent aDNA studies on our view of third millennium Europe. *European Journal of Archaeology, 21,* 159–91, https://doi.org/10.1017/eaa.2017.43.

Galaty, M. L. (2018). *Memory and Nation Building: From Ancient Times to the Islamic State*. Lanham, MD: Rowman & Littlefield.

Gardner, A. (2011). Paradox and praxis in the archaeology of identity. In L. Amundsen-Meyer, N. Engel and S. Pickering, eds., *Identity Crisis: Archaeological Perspectives on Social Identity, Proceedings of the 42nd Annual Chacmool Conference*, Calgary, Alberta, pp. 11–26.

Geller, P. L. (2017). Brave old world: Ancient DNA testing and sex determination. In S. C. Agarwal and J. K. Wesp, eds., *Exploring Sex and Gender in Bioarchaeology*. Albuquerque: University of New Mexico Press, pp. 71–98.

Gilchrist, R. (2000). Archaeological biographies: Realizing human lifecycles,-courses and-histories. *World Archaeology*, *31*(3), 325–28, www.jstor.org/stable/125104.

Gil-White, F. J. (1999). How thick is blood? The plot thickens . . . : If ethnic actors are primordialists, what remains of the circumstantialist/primordialist controversy? *Ethnic and Racial Studies*, *22*(5), 789–820, https://doi.org/10.1080/014198799329260.

Ginn, V., Rebecca E. & Crozier, R., eds. (2014). *Exploring Prehistoric Identity in Europe: Our Construct or Theirs?* Oxford: Oxbow Books.

Gokcumen, O. & Frachetti, M. (2020). The impact of ancient genome studies in archaeology. *Annual Review of Anthropology*, *49*, 277–98, https://doi.org/10.1146/annurev-anthro-010220-074353.

Gokee, C., & De León, J. (2014). Sites of contention. *Journal of Contemporary Archaeology*, *1*, 133–63.

Graeber, D. & Wengrow, D. (2021). *The Dawn of Everything: A New History of Humanity*. London: Penguin.

Graves-Brown, P., Jones, S. & Gamble, C. S., eds. (1996). *Cultural Identity and Archaeology: The Construction of European Communities*, 1st ed., Abingdon: Routledge.

Greenberg, R. & Hamilakis, Y. (2022). *Archaeology, Nation and Race*. Cambridge: Cambridge University Press.

Gretzinger, J., Sayer, D., Justeau, P. et al. (2022). The Anglo-Saxon migration and the formation of the early English gene pool, *Nature*, *610*(7930), 112–19, https://doi.org/10.1038/s41586-022-05247-2.

Haak, W., Brandt, G., Jong, H. N. D. et al. (2008). Ancient DNA, strontium isotopes, and osteological analyses shed light on social and kinship organization of the Later Stone Age. *Proceedings of the National Academy of Sciences*, *105*(47), 18226–31, https://doi.org/10.1073/pnas.0807592105.

Hamilakis, Y. (2007). *The Nation and Its Ruins: Antiquity, Archaeology, and National Imagination in Greece*. Oxford: Oxford University Press.

Handler, J. S. (1997). An African-type healer/diviner and his grave goods: A burial from a plantation slave cemetery in Barbados, West Indies. *International Journal of Historical Archaeology, 1*(2), 91–130, www.jstor.org/stable/ 20852878.

Harrison, R. J. (1974). Origins of the Bell Beaker cultures. *Antiquity, 48*(190), 99–109.

Harrison, R. J. (1980). *The Beaker Folk: Copper Age Archaeology in Western Europe.* London: Thames and Hudson.

Harrison-Buck, E. and Hendon, J. A. eds. 2018. *Relational Identities and Other-Than-Human-Agency in Archaeology.* Louisville:University of Colorado Press.

Hawks, J. (2013). Significance of Neandertal and Denisovan genomes in human evolution. *Annual Review of Anthropology, 42,* 433–49, https://doi.org/ 10.1146/annurev-anthro-092412-155548.

Hayden, B. (2001). Fabulous feasts: A prolegomenon to the importance of feasting. In M. Dietler and B. Hayden, eds., *Feasts: Archaeological and Ethnographic Pespectives on Food, Politics, and Power,* Tuscaloosa: University of Alabama Press, pp. 23–64.

Hayden, B. (2014). *The Power of Feasts: From Prehistory to the Present.* New York: Cambridge University Press.

Heath-Stout, L. E. (2020). Who writes about archaeology? An intersectional study of authorship in archaeological journals. *American Antiquity, 85*(3), 407–26, https://doi.org/10.1017/aaq.2020.28.

Hedenstierna-Jonson, C., Kjellström, A., Zachrisson, T. et al. (2017). A female Viking warrior confirmed by genomics. *American Journal of Physical Anthropology, 164*(4), 853–60, https://doi.org/10.1002/ajpa.23308.

Hedges, R., Bentley, R. A., Bickle, P. et al. (2013). The supra-regional perspective. In P. Bickle and A. Whittle, eds., *The First Farmers in Central Europe: Diversity in LBK Lifeways.* Oxford: Oxbow Books, pp. 343–84.

Herbich, I. (1987). Learning patterns, potter interaction and ceramic style among the Luo of Kenya. *African Archaeological Review, 5*(1), 193–204, www.jstor.org/stable/25130492.

Higgins, D., Rohrlach, A. B., Kaidonis, J., Townsend, G. & Austin, J. J. (2015). Differential nuclear and mitochondrial DNA preservation in post-mortem teeth with implications for forensic and ancient DNA studies. *PloS ONE, 10*(5), 1–17, https://doi.org/10.1371/journal .pone.0126935.

Hobsbawm, E. & Ranger, T., eds. (1983). *The Invention of Tradition.* Cambridge: Cambridge University Press.

Hodder, I. (2000). Agency and individuals in long-term processes. In M. A. Dobres and J. Robb, eds., *Agency in Archaeology*. Abingdon: Routledge, pp. 21–33.

Hodos, T. (2006). *Local Responses to Colonization in the Iron Age Mediterranean*. Abindgon: Routledge.

Hoernes, M. (2022). Staying local: Community formation and resilience in Archaic Southern Sicily. *Journal of Social Archaeology*, *22*(3), 296–316, https://doi.org/10.1177/14696053221114016.

Hollimon, S. (2017). Bioarchaeological approaches to nonbinary genders. In S. Agarwal and J. K. Wesp, eds., *Exploring Sex and Gender in Bioarchaeology*. Albuquerque: University of New Mexico Press, pp. 51–69.

Hope, V. M. (1997). Words and pictures: The interpretation of Romano-British tombstones. *Britannia*, *28*, 245–58, https://doi.org/10.2307/526768.

Hosek, L. & Robb, J. (2019). Osteobiography: A platform for bioarchaeological research. *Bioarchaeology International*, *3*(1), 1, https://doi.org/10.5744/bi.2019.1005.

House, C. M., Caffell, A., Holst, M., Cottage, I. & Wilton, B. (2012). *Osteological Analysis 3 and 6 Driffield Terrace York North Yorkshire*. Aldwark: York Archaeological Trust for Excavation & Research, https://static1.squarespace.com/static/5c62d8bb809d8e27588adcc0/t/5d03951cee83120001608d7b/1560515891116/Osteological+Analysis+3+and+6+Driffield+Terrace+-+Caffell+and+Holst.pdf.

Hubert, J., ed. (2001). *Madness, Disability and Social Exclusion: The Archaeology and Anthropology of "Difference,"* 1st ed., Abingdon: Routledge.

identity, n. (2023). *Oxford English Dictionary*. Oxford University Press, https://doi.org/10.1093/OED/8369890298.

Ingold, T. (2007). *Lines: A Brief History*. Abingdon: Routledge.

Insoll, T., ed. (2007). *The Archaeology of Identities: A Reader*. Abingdon: Routledge.

Jamieson, R. W. (1995). Material culture and social death: African-American burial practices. *Historical Archaeology*, *29*(40), 39–58.

Jamieson, R. W. (2005). Caste in Cuenca: Colonial identity in the seventeenth century Andes. In E. Casella and C. Fowler, eds., *The Archaeology of Plural and Changing Identities: Beyond Identification*. Boston, MA: Springer US EBooks, pp. 211–32, https://doi.org/10.1007/0-306-48695-4_10.

Jenkins, R. (1996). *Social Identity*, 1st ed., Abingdon: Routledge.

Johannsen, N. N., Larson, G., Meltzer, D. J. & Vander Linden, M. (2017). A composite window into human history: Better integration of ancient DNA studies with archaeology promises deeper insights. *Science*, *356*(6343), 1118–20, https://doi.org/10.1126/science.aan0737.

Johnson, K. M., & Paul, K. S. (2016). Bioarchaeology and kinship: integrating theory, social relatedness, and biology in ancient family research. *Journal of Archaeological Research, 24,* 75–123.

Jørkov, M. L. S., Jørgensen, L., & Lynnerup, N. (2010). Uniform diet in a diverse society. Revealing new dietary evidence of the Danish Roman Iron Age based on stable isotope analysis. *American Journal of Physical Anthropology, 143*(4), 523–33.

Jones, A. M. (2012). *Prehistoric Materialities: Becoming Material in Prehistoric Britain and Ireland.* Oxford: Oxford University Press.

Jones, S. (1997). *The Archaeology of Ethnicity: Constructing Identities in the Past and Present.* Abingdon: Routledge.

Jones, A. M. & Hamilakis, Y. (2017). Archaeology and assemblage. *Cambridge Archaeological Journal, 27*(1), 77–84, https://doi.org/10.1017/S095977431 6000688.

Joyce, R. A. (2017). Sex, gender, and anthropology. In S. Agarwal and J. K. Wesp, eds., *Exploring Sex and Gender in Bioarchaeology.* Albuquerque: University of New Mexico Press, pp. 1–14.

Juras, A., Chyleński, M., Krenz-Niedbała, M. et al. (2017). Investigating kinship of Neolithic post-LBK remains from Krusza Zamkowa, Poland using ancient DNA. *Forensic Science International: Genetics, 26,* 30–39.

Keane, W. (2003). Semiotics and the social analysis of material things. *Language & Communication, 23*(3–4), 409–25, https://doi.org/10.1016/ S0271-5309(03)00010-7.

Klima, B. (1987). A triple burial from the Upper Paleolithic of Dolní Věstonice, Czechoslovakia. *Journal of Human Evolution, 16*(7–8), 831–35.

Knapp, A. B. (2021). *Migration Myths and the End of the Bronze Age in the Eastern Mediterranean.* Cambridge: Cambridge University Press.

Knipper, C., Meyer, C., Jacobi, F. et al. (2014). Social differentiation and land use at an early Iron Age "princely seat": Bioarchaeological investigations at the Glauberg (Germany). *Journal of Archaeological Science, 41,* 818–35, https://doi.org/10.1016/j.jas.2013.09.019.

Knudson, K. J. & Stojanowski, C. M. (2008). New directions in bioarchaeology: Recent contributions to the study of human social identities. *Journal of Archaeological Research, 16*(4), 397–432, https://doi.org/ 10.1007/s10814-008-9024-4.

Kohn, E. 2015. Anthropology of ontologies. *Annual Review of Anthropology,* 44, 311–27.

Kotsakis, K. (2003). Ideological aspects of contemporary archaeology in Greece. In M. Haagsma, ed., *The Impact of Classical Greece on European*

74 References

and National Identities, Leiden: Brill, pp. 55–70. https://doi.org/10.1163/9789004502277_006.

Kramer, C. & Stark, M. (1994). The status of women in archeology. *Archeological Papers of the American Anthropological Association*, 5(1), 17–22, https://doi.org/10.1525/ap3a.1994.5.1.17.

Kristiansen, K. (2014). Towards a new paradigm? The third science revolution and its possible consequences in archaeology. *Current Swedish Archaeology*, 22(1), 11–34, https://doi.org/10.37718/CSA.2014.01.

Kristiansen, K. (2022). *Archaeology and the Genetic Revolution in European Prehistory* (Elements in the Archaeology of Europe). Cambridge: Cambridge University Press, https://doi.org/10.1017/9781009228701.

Krutak, L. (2019). Therapeutic tattooing in the Arctic: Ethnographic, archaeological, and ontological frameworks of analysis. *International Journal of Paleopathology*, 25, 99–109, https://doi.org/10.1016/j.ijpp.2018.05.003.

Kuhn, T. S. (1996). *The Structure of Scientific Revolutions*, 3rd ed. Chicago, IL: University of Chicago Press.

Larsen, M. T. (1989). Orientalism and near eastern archaeology. In D. Miller, M. Rowlands and C. Tilley, eds., *Domination and Resistance*. Abingdon: Routledge, pp. 228–38.

Latour, B. (2005). *Reassembling the Social: An Introduction to Actor-Network-Theory*. Oxford: Oxford University Press.

Laurence, R. & Berry, J., eds. (1998). *Cultural Identity in the Roman Empire*. Abingdon: Routledge.

LeCount, L. J. (2010). Maya palace kitchens: Suprahousehold food preparation at the late classic Maya site of Xunantunich. In E. Klarich, ed., *Inside Ancient Kitchens: New Directions in the Study of Daily Meals and Feasts*, Boulder: University of Colorado Press, pp. 133–62.

Lehner, M. (2002). The pyramid age settlement of the southern mount at Giza. *Journal of the American Research Center in Egypt*, 39, 27–74, https://doi.org/10.2307/40001149.

Le Huray, J. & Schutkowski, H. (2005). Diet and social status during the La Tène period in Bohemia: Carbon and nitrogen stable isotope analysis of bone collagen from Kutná Hora-Karlov and Radovesice. *Journal of Anthropological Archaeology*, 24(2), 135–147, https://doi.org/10.1016/j.jaa.2004.09.002.

Leone, M. P. (1984). Interpreting ideology in historical archaeology: Using the rules of perspective in the William Paca Garden in Annapolis, Maryland. In D. Miller and C. Tilley, eds., *Ideology, Power, and Prehistory*. Cambridge: Cambridge University Press, pp. 25–35.

Leppard, T. P., Esposito, C. & Esposito, M. (2020). The bioarchaeology of migration in the ancient Mediterranean: Meta-analysis of radiogenic (87Sr/86Sr) isotope ratios. *Journal of Mediterranean Archaeology*, *33*, 211–41, https://doi.org/10.1558/jma.18784.

Lilley, I. (2004). Diaspora and identity in archaeology: Moving beyond the Black Atlantic. In L. Meskell and R. W. Preucel, eds., *A Companion to Social Archaeology*, Oxford: Blackwell, pp. 287–312, https://doi.org/10.1002/9780470693605.ch13.

Lilley, I. (2006). Archaeology, diaspora and decolonization. *Journal of Social Archaeology*, *6*(1), 28–47, https://doi.org/10.1177/1469605306060560.

Lillios, K. T. (1999). Objects of memory: The ethnography and archaeology of heirlooms. *Journal of Archaeological Method and Theory*, *6*(3), 235–62, www.jstor.org/stable/20177404.

Ling, R., Arthur, P., Clarke, G. et al. (1997). I 10, 7: Casa del Fabbro. In R. Ling, ed., *The Insula of the Menander at Pompeii: Volume 1: The Structures*, Oxford: Oxford Academic, pp. 150–170, https://doi.org/10.1093/oso/9780198134091.003.0019.

Lobo, I. & Zhaurova, K. (2008) Birth defects: Causes and statistics. *Nature Education*, *1*(1), 18, www.nature.com/scitable/topicpage/birth-defects-causes-and-statistics-863/.

López Ruíz, C. (2021). *Phoenicians and the Making of the Mediterranean*. Boston, MA: Harvard University Press.

Maldonado, A. & Russell, A. (2016). Introduction: Creating material worlds. In L. Campbell, A. Maldonado, E. Pierce and A. Russell, eds., *Creating Material Worlds: The Uses of Identity in Archaeology*. Oxford: Oxbow Books, pp. 1–15.

Malkin, I. (1998). *The Returns of Odysseus: Colonization and Ethnicity*. Berkeley: University of California Press.

Manasterski, D., Januszek, K., Wawrusiewicz, A. & Klecha, A. (2020). Bell Beaker cultural package in the east European periphery of the Phenomenon: A case of ritual features in north-eastern Poland. *Documenta Praehistorica*, *47*, 374–89, https://doi.org/10.4312/dp.47.20.

Maran, J. (2022). Archaeological cultures, fabricated ethnicities and DNA research: "Minoans" and "Mycenaeans" as case examples. In U. Davidovich, N. Yahalom-Mack and S. Matskevich, eds., *Material, Method, and Meaning: Papers in Eastern Mediterranean Archaeology in Honor of Ilan Sharon*. Ägypten und Altes Testament 110, Münster: Zaphon, pp. 7–25.

Martin, D. (n.d.). *Bioarchaeology and Social Theory*. Book series, New York: Springer. www.springer.com/series/11976.

Martin, S. C. (2023). Materiality in transit: An ethnographic-archaeological approach to objects carried, lost, and gained during contemporary migration journeys. *Journal of Social Archaeology, 23*(1), 3–24, https://doi.org10.1177/14696053221144754.

Masclans Latorre, A., Bickle, P. & Hamon, C. (2021). Sexual inequalities in the early Neolithic? Exploring relationships between sexes/genders at the cemetery of Vedrovice using use-wear analysis, diet and mobility. *Journal of Archaeological Method and Theory, 28*(1), 232–73, https://doi.org/10.1007/s10816-020-09453-y.

Mattingly, D. J. (2014). *Imperialism, Power, and Identity: Experiencing the Roman Empire*. Princeton, NJ: Princeton University Press.

McGuire, R. H. (1992). *A Marxist Archaeology*. San Diego, CA: Academic Press.

McPherson, M., Smith-Lovin, L. & Cook, J. M. (2001). Birds of a feather: Homophily in social networks. *Annual Review of Sociology, 27*, 415–44, https://doi.org/10.1146/annurev.soc.27.1.415.

Merkl, M. B. (2010). Bell Beaker metallurgy and the emergence of fahlore-copper use in Central Europe. *Interdisciplinaria Archaeologica, 1*, 19–27.

Meskell, L. (1996). The somatization of archaeology: Institutions, discourses, corporeality. *Norwegian Archaeological Review, 29*(1), 1–16, https://doi.org/10.1080/00293652.1996.9965595.

Meskell, L. M. (2001). Archaeologies of identity. In I. Hodder, ed., *Archaeological Theory: Breaking the Boundaries*. Cambridge: Polity Press, pp. 187–213.

Meskell, L., ed. (2002). *Archaeology under Fire: Nationalism, Politics and Heritage in the Eastern Mediterranean and Middle East*. Abingdon: Routledge.

Meskell, L., ed. (2008). *Archaeologies of Materiality*. Hoboken, NJ: John Wiley & Sons.

Meyer, C., Ganslmeier, R., Dresely, V. & Alt, K. W. (2012). New approaches to the reconstruction of kinship and social structure based on bioarchaeological analysis of Neolithic multiple and collective graves. In J. Kolář and F. Trampota, eds., *Theoretical and Methodological Considerations in Central European Neolithic Archaeology*. British Archaeological Reports International Series 2325, Oxford: Archaeopress, pp. 11–23.

Miller, D., Rowlands, M. & Tilley, C., eds. (1989). *Domination and Resistance*. London: Unwin Hyman.

Mirza, M. N. & Dungworth, D. B. (1995). The potential misuse of genetic analyses and the social construction of "race" and "ethnicity." *Oxford*

Journal of Archaeology, *14*(3), 345–54, https://doi.org/10.1111/j.1468-0092.1995.tb00068.x.

Mittnik, A. & Krause, J. (2016). Genetic analysis of the Dolní Věstonice human remains. In J. Svoboda, ed., *Dolní Věstonice II: Chronostratigraphy, Paleoethnology, Paleoanthropology Dolní Věstonice Studies,* Brno: Academy of Sciences of the Czech Republic, pp. 377–84.

Mittnik, A., Wang, C.-C., Svoboda, J. & Krause, J. (2016). A molecular approach to the sexing of the triple burial at the upper paleolithic site of Dolní Věstonice. *PLoS ONE,* *11*(10), 1–9, https://doi.org/10.1371/journal.pone.0163019.

Mittnik, A., Massy, K., Knipper, C. et al. (2019). Kinship-based social inequality in Bronze Age Europe. *Science,* *366*(6466), 731–34, https://doi.org/10.1126/science.aax6219.

Mol, E. (2018). Review of *Creating Material Worlds: The Uses of Identity in Archaeology,* A. Russell, E. Pierce, A. Maldonado and L. Campbell, eds. *Cambridge Archaeological Journal,* *28*(4), 723–24, https://doi.org/10.1017/S0959774318000082.

Montón-Subías, S. & Meyer, W. (2014). Engendered archaeologies. In C. Smith, ed., *Encyclopedia of Global Archaeology.* New York: Springer, https://doi.org/10.1007/978-1-4419-0465-2_259.

Moore, H. L. (1994). *A Passion for Difference: Essays in Anthropology and Gender.* Bloomington: Indiana University Press.

Moore, J. & Scott, E., eds. (1997). *Invisible People and Processes: Writing Gender and Childhood into European Archaeology.* London: Leicester University Press.

Müldner, G., Chenery, C. & Eckardt, H. (2011). The "Headless Romans": Multi-isotope investigations of an unusual burial ground from Roman Britain. *Journal of Archaeological Science,* *38,* 280–90, https://doi.org/10.1016/j.jas.2010.09.003.

Müldner, G., Britton, K. & Ervynck, A. (2014). Inferring animal husbandry strategies in coastal zones through stable isotope analysis: New evidence from the Flemish coastal plain (Belgium, 1st–15th century AD). *Journal of Archaeological Science,* *42,* 322–32, https://doi.org/10.1016/j.jas.2013.08.010.

Müller, W., Fricke, H., Halliday, A. N., McCulloch, M. T. & Wartho, J. A. (2003). Origin and migration of the Alpine Iceman. *Science,* *302*(5646), 862–66, https://doi.org/10.1126/science.1089837.

Nehlich, O. (2015). The application of sulphur isotope analyses in archaeological research: A review. *Earth-Science Reviews,* *142,* 1–17, https://doi.org/10.1016/j.earscirev.2014.12.002.

Nevett, L. C. (2001). *House and Society in the Ancient Greek World*. Cambridge: Cambridge University Press.

Niklasson, E. (2014). Shutting the stable door after the horse has bolted: Critical thinking and the third science revolution. *Current Swedish Archaeology, 22*, 57–63, https://doi.org/10.37718/CSA.2014.06.

Notarian, M. (2023). A spatial network analysis of water distribution from public fountains in Pompeii. *American Journal of Archaeology, 127*(1), 85–118, https://doi.org/10.1086/722233.

Olalde, I., Brace, S., Allentoft, M. E. et al. (2018). The Beaker phenomenon and the genomic transformation of northwest Europe. *Nature, 555*(7695), 190–96.

Olsen, B. (2007). Keeping things at arm's length: A genealogy of asymmetry. *World Archaeology, 39*(4), 579–88, www.jstor.org/stable/40026150.

Olsen, B., Shanks, M., Webmoor, T. & Witmore, C. (2012). *Archaeology: The Discipline of Things*. Berkeley: University of California Press.

Papalexandrou, A. (2003). Memory tattered and torn: Spolia in the heartland of Byzantine Hellenism. In R. M. Van Dyke and S. E. Alcock, eds., *Archaeologies of Memory*. Hoboken, NJ: John Wiley & Sons, pp. 56–80.

Parker Pearson, M. (1982). Mortuary practices, society, and ideology: An ethnoarchaeological case study. In I. Hodder, ed., *Symbolic and Structural Archaeology*. Cambridge: Cambridge University Press, pp. 99–113.

Pearson, J. A. (2013). Human and animal diet as evidenced by stable carbon and nitrogen isotope analysis. In I. Hodder (Ed.), *Humans and Landscapes of Çatalhöyük: Reports from the 2000–2008 Seasons* (pp. 271–298). Los Angeles: Cotsen Institute.

Pearson, J., & Meskell, L. (2015). Isotopes and images: fleshing out bodies at Çatalhöyük. *Journal of Archaeological Method and Theory, 22*, 461–82.

Peeples, M. A. (2018). *Connected Communities: Social Networks, Identity, and Social Change in the Ancient Cibola World*. Tucson: University of Arizona Press.

Peintner, U. & Pöder, R. (2000). Ethnomycological remarks on the Iceman's fungi. In S. Bortenschlager and K. Oeggl, eds., *The Iceman and His Natural Environment: The Man in the Ice*, Vol 4, Vienna: Springer Vienna, pp. 143–50.

Perry, M. A., Killgrove, K., Gregoricka, L. A. & Prowse, T. L. (2022). Mediterranean bioarchaeology, meta-analysis and migration: Towards accurate meta-analyses in Mediterranean bioarchaeology: A critical response to Leppard et al. (*JMA 33*, 2020). *Journal of Mediterranean Archaeology, 35*(1), 108–32, https://doi.org/10.1558/jma.23771.

Pilloud, M. A. & Larsen, C. S. (2011). "Official" and "practical" kin: Inferring social and community structure from dental phenotype at Neolithic Çatalhöyük, Turkey. *American Journal of Physical Anthropology, 145*(4), 519–30, https://doi.org/10.1002/ajpa.21520.

Politis, G. & Saunders, N. (2002). Archaeological correlates of ideological activity: Food taboos and spirit-animals in an Amazonian hunter-gatherer society. In N. Milner and P. Miracle, eds., *Consuming Passions and Patterns of Consumption*, Cambridge: McDonald Institute, pp. 113–30.

Price, N., Hedenstierna-Jonson, C., Zachrisson, T. et al. (2019). Viking warrior women? Reassessing Birka chamber grave Bj. 581. *Antiquity, 93*(367), 181–98, https://doi.org/10.15184/aqy.2018.258.

Rebillard, E. (2015). Material culture and religious identity in Late Antiquity. In R. Raja and J. Rüpke, eds., *A Companion to the Archaeology of Religion in the Ancient World*. Hoboken, NJ: John Wiley & Sons, pp. 425–36.

Reckner, P. E. & Brighton, S. A. (1999). "Free from All Vicious Habits": Archaeological perspectives on class conflict and the rhetoric of temperance. *Historical Archaeology, 1999, 33*(1), 63–86, www.jstor.org/stable/25616672.

Reich, D. (2018). *Who We Are and How We Got Here: Ancient DNA and the New Science of the Human Past*. London: Pantheon.

Richards, M. P., Hedges, R. E., Molleson, T. I., & Vogel, J. C. (1998). Stable isotope analysis reveals variations in human diet at the Poundbury Camp cemetery site. *Journal of Archaeological Science, 25*(12), 1247–52.

Richards, M., Smith, C., Nehlich, O. et al. (2022). Finding Mycenaeans in Minoan Crete? Isotope and DNA analysis of human mobility in Bronze Age Crete. *PloS ONE, 17*(8), 1–22, https://doi.org/10.1371/journal.pone.0272144.

Rott, E. (2000). Diatoms from the colon of the Iceman. In S. Bortenschlager and K. Oeggl, eds., *The Iceman and His Natural Environment: The Man in the Ice*, Vol 4, Vienna: Springer Vienna, pp. 117–25.

Roymans, N. (2019). Conquest, mass violence and ethnic stereotyping: Investigating Caesar's actions in the Germanic frontier zone. *Journal of Roman Archaeology, 32*, 439–58. https://doi.org/10.1017/S1047759419000229.

Russell, A., Pierce, E., Maldonado, A. & Campbell, L., eds. (2016). *Creating Material Worlds: The Uses of Identity in Archaeology*. Oxford: Oxbow Books.

Sahlins, M. (2013). *What Kinship Is—And Is Not*. Chicago: University of Chicago Press.

Samadelli, M., Melis, M., Miccoli, M., Vigl, E. E. & Zink, A. R. (2015). Complete mapping of the tattoos of the 5300-year-old Tyrolean Iceman.

Journal of Cultural Heritage, 16(5), 753–58, https://doi.org/10.1016/j.culher.2014.12.005.

Schoeninger, M. J. & Moore, K. (1992). Bone stable isotope studies in archaeology. *Journal of World Prehistory, 6,* 247–96, https://doi.org/10.1007/BF00975551.

Schutkowski, H., Herrmann, B., Wiedemann, F., Bocherens, H. & Grupe, G. (1999). Diet, status and decomposition at Weingarten: Trace element and isotopic analyses on Early Medieval skeletal material. *Journal of Archaeological Science, 26,* 675–85, https://doi.org/10.1006/jasc.1998.0384.

Schweissing M. M., & Grupe, G. (2003). Stable strontium isotopes in human teeth and bone: A key to migration events of the late Roman period in Bavaria. *Journal of Archeological Science, 30*(11), 1373–83, https://doi.org/10.1016/S0305-4403(03)00025-6.

Scorrano, G., Viva, S., Pinotti, T., et al. (2022). Bioarchaeological and palaeogenomic portrait of two Pompeians that died during the eruption of Vesuvius in 79 AD. *Scientific Reports, 12*(1), 1–12.

Semerari, G. S., Kyle, B., & Reitsema, L. (2021). Perils, Potential and Perspectives of Bioarchaeological Analyses in the Study of Mediterranean Mobility. *Journal of Mediterranean Archaeology, 34*(1), 84–108.

Shay, T. (1985). Differentiated treatment of deviancy at death as revealed in anthropological and archeological material. *Journal of Anthropological Archaeology, 4*(3), 221–41, https://doi.org/10.1016/0278-4165(85)90004-2.

Sherratt, A. (1987). Cups that cheered. In W. H. Waldren and R. C. Kennard, eds., *Bell Beakers of the Western Mediterranean: Definition, Interpretation, Theory and New Site Data.* Oxford: British Archaeological Reports, International Series S331, pp. 81–114.

Sikora, M., Carpenter, M. L., Moreno-Estrada, A. et al. (2014). Population genomic analysis of ancient and modern genomes yields new insights into the genetic ancestry of the Tyrolean Iceman and the genetic structure of Europe. *PLoS Genetics, 10*(5), 1–12, https://doi.org/10.1371/journal.pgen.1004353.

Sikora, M., Seguin-Orlando, A., Sousa, V. C. et al. (2017). Ancient genomes show social and reproductive behaviour of early upper paleolithic foragers. *Science, 358*(6363), 659–62, www.science.org/doi/10.1126/science.aao1807.

Sjögren, K. G. & Price, T. D. (2013). A complex Neolithic economy: Isotope evidence for the circulation of cattle and sheep in the TRB of western Sweden. *Journal of Archeological Science, 40,* 690–704, https://doi.org/10.1016/j.jas.2012.08.001.

Sjögren, K. G., Price, T. D. & Ahlström, T. (2009). Megaliths and mobility in southwestern Sweden: Investigating relations between a local society and its neighbours using strontium isotopes. *Journal of Anthropological Archaeology*, *28*, 85–101, https://doi.org/10.1016/J.JAA.2008.10.001.

Slon, V, Hopfe, C., Weiß, C. et al. (2017). Neandertal and Denisovan DNA from Pleistocene sediments. *Science*, *356*, 605–608, https://doi.org/10.1126/science.aam9695.

Sofaer, J. R. (2006). *The Body as Material Culture: A Theoretical Osteoarchaeology* (Topics in Contemporary Archaeology). Cambridge: Cambridge University Press, https://doi.org/10.1017/CBO9780511816666.

Soren, D., Fenton, T. & Birkby, W. (1995). The late Roman infant cemetery near Lugnano in Teverina, Italy: Some implications. *Journal of Paleopathology, 7*, 13–42.

Soriano, I., Herrero-Corral, A. M., Garrido-Pena, R. & Majó, T. (2021). Sex/gender system and social hierarchization in Bell Beaker burials from Iberia. *Journal of Anthropological Archaeology*, *64*, 1–15, https://doi.org/10.1016/j.jaa.2021.101335.

Souvatzi, S. (2017). Kinship and social archaeology. *Cross-Cultural Research*, *51*(2), 172–95, https://doi.org/10.1177/1069397117691028.

Spencer-Wood, S. M., Trunzo, J. M. C., & Woehlke, S., eds. (2022). Special issue on intersectionality theory and research in historical archaeology. *Archaeologies*, *18*, 1–44, https://doi.org/10.1007/s11759-022-09442-5.

Spindler, K. (1995). *The Man in the Ice: The Preserved Body of a Neolithic Man Reveals the Secrets of the Stone Age*. Translated by Ewald Osers. London: Harmony Books.

Stone, R. (2000). Ice Man warms up for European scientists. *Science, 289* (5488), 2253–54, https://doi.org/10.1126/science.289.5488.2253a.

Strathern, M. (1988). *The Gender of the Gift: Problems with Women and Problems with Society in Melanesia*. Berkeley, CA: University of California Press.

Svoboda, J. (2006). The burials: Ritual and taphonomy. In E. Trinkaus and J. Svoboda, eds., *Early Modern Human Evolution in Central Europe: The People of Dolní Věstonice and Pavlov*. Oxford: Oxford University Press, pp. 15–26.

Svoboda, J. (2020). *Dolní Vestonice–Pavlov: Explaining Paleolithic Settlements in Central Europe*. Translated by S. Dibble. College Station, TX: Texas A&M University Press.

Sykes, N., Spriggs, M. & Evin, A. (2019). Beyond curse or blessing: The opportunities and challenges of aDNA analysis. *World Archaeology, 51*(4), 503–16, https://doi.org/10.1080/00438243.2019.1741970.

Szostek, K., Czech, K. and Cienkosz-Stepańczak, B. (2015). Strontium isotopes as an indicator of human migration: Easy questions, difficult answers. *Anthropological Review, 78*(2), 133–56.

Tafuri, M. A., Craig, O. E., & Canci, A. (2009). Stable isotope evidence for the consumption of millet and other plants in Bronze Age Italy. *American Journal of Physical Anthropology: The Official Publication of the American Association of Physical Anthropologists, 139*(2), 146–53.

Tarlow, S. (2007). The archaeology of identities: A reader. *Public Archaeology, 6*(2), 129–32, https://doi.org/10.1179/175355307X230766.

Thomas, J. (2006). Gene-flows and social processes: The potential of genetics and archaeology. *Documenta praehistorica, 33*, 51–59.

Todd, Z. (2016). An Indigenous feminist's take on the ontological turn: "Ontology" is just another word for colonialism. *Journal of Historical Sociology, 29*(1), 4–22, https://doi.org/10.1111/johs.12124.

Tringham, R. (1991). Households with faces: The challenge of gender in prehistoric architectural remains. In J. Gero and M. Conkey, eds., *Engendering Archaeology: Women and Prehistory*. Hoboken, NJ: Wiley-Blackwell, pp. 93–131.

Trinkaus, E., Buzhilova, A. P., Mednikova, M. B. & Dobrovolskaya, M. V. (2014). *The People of Sunghir: Burials, Bodies and Behavior in the Earlier Upper Palaeolithic*. Oxford: Oxford University Press.

Trinkaus, E., Formicola, V., Svoboda, J., Hillson, S. W. & Holliday, T. W. (2001). Dolní Věstonice 15: Pathology and persistence in the Pavlovian. *Journal of Archaeological Science, 28*(12), 1291–308, https://doi.org/10.1006/jasc.2001.0678.

Trinkaus, E., Svoboda, J. A., Wojtal, P., Fišáková, M. N. & Wilczyński, J. (2010). Human remains from the Moravian Gravettian: Morphology and taphonomy of additional elements from Dolní Věstonice II and Pavlov I. *International Journal of Osteoarchaeology, 20*(6), 645–69, https://doi.org/10.1002/oa.1088.

Uprichard, E. & Dawney, L. (2019). Data diffraction: Challenging data integration in mixed methods research. *Journal of Mixed Methods Research, 13*(1), 19–32, https://doi.org/10.1177/1558689816674650.

Van der Veen, M. (2003). When is food a luxury? *World Archaeology, 34*(3), 405–27, www.jstor.org/stable/3560194.

Van Dyke, R. M. (2021). Ethics, not objects. *Cambridge Archaeological Journal, 31*(3), 487–93, https://doi.org/10.1017/S0959774321000172.

Van Dyke, R. M. & Alcock, S. E., eds. (2003). *Archaeologies of Memory*. Hoboken, NJ: John Wiley.

Vaňharová, M. & Drozdová, E. (2008). Sex determination of skeletal remains of 4000 year old children and juveniles from Hoštice 1 za Hanou (Czech Republic) by ancient DNA analysis. *Anthropological Review, 71*(1), 63–70, https://doi.org10.2478/v10044-008-0011-7.

Vidal-Ronchas, R., Rajić Šikanjić, P., Premuzic, Z., Papeša, A., & Lightfoot, E. (2019). Diet, sex, and social status in the Late Avar period: Stable isotope investigations at Nuštar cemetery, Croatia. *Archaeological and Anthropological Sciences, 11*, 1727–37. https://doi.org/10.1007/s12520-018-0628-4.

Viveiros de Castro, E. (1998). Cosmological deixis and amerindian perspectivism. *Journal of the Royal Anthropological Institute, 4*(3), 469–88, https://doi.org/10.2307/3034157.

Voss, B. L. (2000). Feminisms, queer theories, and the archaeological study of past sexualities. *World Archaeology, 32*(2), 180–92, www.jstor.org/stable/827864.

Voss, B. L. (2008). Sexuality studies in archaeology. *Annual Review of Anthropology, 37*, 317–36, https://doi.org/10.1146/annurev.anthro.37.081407.085238.

Wang, K., Prüfer, K., Krause-Kyora, B. et al. (2023). High-coverage genome of the Tyrolean Iceman reveals unusually high Anatolian Farmer Ancestry. *Cell Genomics, 3*, 1–8, https://doi.org/10.1016/j.xgen.2023.100377.

Wells, P. S. (2001). *Beyond Celts, Germans and Scythians: Archaeology and Identity in Iron Age Europe*. London: Duckworth.

Wenger, E. (1998). *Communities of Practice: Learning, Meaning, and Identity*. Cambridge: Cambridge University Press.

Williams, H. (1998). Monuments and the past in early Anglo-Saxon England. *World Archaeology, 30*(1), 90–108, www.jstor.org/stable/125011.

Willman, J. C. (2016). Dental wear at Dolní Věstonice II: Habitual behaviors and social identities written on teeth. *Dolnı Věstonice II: Chronostratigraphy, Paleoethnology, Paleoanthropology Dolnı Věstonice Studies, 21*, 353–371, https://doi.org/10.1371/journal.pone.0224573.

Wilson, J. A. (2022). Negotiating Infant Personhood in Death: Interpreting Atypical Burials in the Late Roman Infant and Child Cemetery at Poggio Gramignano (Italy). *American Journal of Archaeology, 126*(2), 219–41.

Wright, R. P., ed. (1996). *Gender and Archaeology*. Philadelphia: University of Pennsylvania Press.

Zembylas, M. (2017). The contribution of the ontological turn in education: Some methodological and political implications. *Educational Philosophy and Theory, 49*(14), 1401–14. https://doi.org/10.1080/00131857.2017.1309636.

Cambridge Elements ☰

Anthropological Archaeology in the 21st Century

Eli Dollarhide

New York University Abu Dhabi

Eli Dollarhide is an archaeological anthropologist who specializes in the prehistory of the Middle East with a focus on the Persian Gulf. His research investigates the role of small and rural settlements in the development of Bronze Age exchange networks and political systems. Dollarhide co-directs research at the UNESCO World Heritage Site of Bat, Oman and investigates ancient ceramic technologies. See: https://nyuad.nyu.edu/en/research/faculty-labs-and-projects/humanities-research-fellowship-program/research-fellows/eli-dollarhide.html.

Michael Galaty

University of Michigan

Michael Galaty is Professor of Anthropology in the Department of Anthropology and Director and Curator of European and Mediterranean Archaeology in the Museum of Anthropological Archaeology at the University of Michigan. He conducts fieldwork in Albania, Greece, and Kosovo, with a focus on the prehistoric origins of social inequalities. To that end, he utilizes intensive regional surveys and targeted excavations, along with various laboratory techniques, to track the changing economic and political factors that lead to transformative changes in Mediterranean and Balkan social systems, during the Bronze Age, in particular, mgalaty@umich.edu.

Junko Habu

University of California, Berkeley

Junko Habu is Professor of Anthropology and Chair of the Center for Japanese Studies, University of California, Berkeley, and Affiliate Professor of the Research Institute for Humanity and Nature. She has published extensively on Japanese and East Asian archaeology, hunter-gatherer archaeology, and historical ecology. Her current research focuses on the intersection of archeology, agroecology, and traditional ecological knowledge to consider the resilience of socioeconomic systems in the past, present, and future. For more information, see https://junkohabu.com/

Patricia A. McAnany

University of North Carolina at Chapel Hill

Patricia A. McAnany, Kenan Eminent Professor and Chair of Anthropology at the University of North Carolina at Chapel Hill, is co-director of Proyecto Arqueológico Colaborativo del Oriente de Yucatán – a community-archaeology project at Tahcabo, Yucatán, México. She co-founded and directs InHerit: Indigenous Heritage Passed to Present (www.in-herit.org) a UNC program that generates collaborative research and education projects focused on archaeology and cultural heritage with communities in the Maya region and North Carolina. She is the author of several books (most recently Maya Cultural Heritage: How Archaeologists and Indigenous Peoples Engage the Past) as well as journal articles and book chapters on a range of archaeological and heritage topics.

John K. Millhauser

North Carolina State University

John K. Millhauser is an Associate Professor of Anthropology in the Department of Sociology and Anthropology at North Carolina State University. His archaeological work in Mexico centers on rural communities and social economies under Mexica and Spanish rule. His current research integrates economic anthropology and political ecology to better understand the origins of poverty and structural violence. For more information, visit chass .ncsu.edu/people/jkmillha/

Rita Wright

New York University

Rita Wright, Professor Emerita of Anthropology at New York University. Using Near Eastern texts as secondary sources and ancient technologies (ceramics and weaving), she investigates divisions of labor and women's contributions to history. In the field, she has conducted research in Afghanistan, Pakistan, and Iran, predominately in Baluchistan at Mehrgarh and the Punjab, Pakistan, at the city of Harappa. Her Landscape and Settlement survey of Harappa's rural areas is the first conducted in studies of the Indus civilization. She is the founder and editor of Cambridge University Press, Case Studies in Early Societies, especially Ancient Indus: Urbanism, Economy, and Society (Cambridge University Press, 2010).

About the Series

This Element offers anthropological and contemporary perspectives in the study of prehistoric and historic societies globally and cutting-edge research with balanced coverage of well-known sites and understudied times and places. We solicit contributions based on three themes: 1. new methods and technologies producing fresh understandings of the past; 2. theoretical approaches challenging basic concepts and offering new insights; 3. archaeological responses for the 21st century providing informed choices for the present. Individual volumes focus on specific sites and regions that highlight the diversity of human experience around the world and across history which include scholars working throughout North America, Mesoamerica, Europe and the Mediterranean, Africa, the Middle East, and South and East Asia and readers with an avid interest in the latest frontiers in archaeological thought. The media-rich volumes will be an important resource for students, scholars.

Cambridge Elements ≡

Anthropological Archaeology in the 21st Century

Elements in the Series

A full series listing is available at: www.cambridge.org/EATF

Printed in the United States
by Baker & Taylor Publisher Services